Hindu Philosophy for an Inquisitive Mind

The Whats, Hows and Whys...

Title: Hindu Philosophy for an Inquisitive Mind

Author: Siddharth Bhaskar
Twitter: @_SatChitAnanda_

Acknowledgements

So often it's just the author who gets the credit for writing a book even though there are so many others involved without whom the book could never take the shape it finally does. The same is true in my case as I have been helped immensely by friends and family all through the journey of writing my first book.

Firstly, I would have never thought of writing this book without the encouragement and prodding from my friend Sanjan Sarin. Once I started this journey, others came along to help me with ideas, thoughts, criticism, questions, suggestions, and so on. Every bit helped. Perhaps the most comprehensive set of feedback and support came from my father Pramod K. Mishra and my friend Puneet Khurana. Being a first-time author, I took help from so many to gather confidence in what I was writing :) My friends and family didn't disappoint at those key junctures. Quite specifically, I must thank Vaibhav Sharma, Kadambari Jha and Nidhi Satish for taking time out to review my drafts and share feedback. Yash Khanna and Sonali Jha, your encouragement helped way more than you can ever imagine. Thank you so much.

Of course, this acknowledgement can't end without thanking my wife, Anushka, who had to bear both my lost presence as well as my frequent absence

while I was focused on completing this book.
Needless to say, her love and support was
instrumental in getting me this far.

Thank you all for making this a reality.

एकं सद्विप्रां बहुधा वंदन्त्यग्निं
The truth is one, sages call it differently
-    *Rig Veda*

Table of Contents

Chapter 1 - Introduction

Thanks for picking up this book! I assume that you are interested in the Hindu philosophy or may be interested in religious philosophies, in general. Let me take this opportunity to briefly tell you what to expect in this book.

People turn to religion for various reasons - some see it as the path of righteousness, a guide that tells you - what is right and what is wrong... what is good and what is evil; some see it as a way to get rid of all sufferings and miseries and anxieties and stresses of this world; some look at it to find the ultimate purpose of life; some see it as divine knowledge, some as mystic knowledge; and some even see it as a placebo to keep people in a state of delusion!

In this book, we will try to explore all these topics and more, from the standpoint of the Hindu philosophy. We will identify and discuss the key philosophical ideas of Hinduism, and hopefully, do it in a way that is logical and easy to comprehend.

Hey, wait a minute did I say "Hinduism"? Well, I must admit here that Hindu and Hinduism are rather modern constructs. Whenever I mention Hinduism, what I am referring to is the *Sanatana Dharma* which is often translated as the eternal way of life.

So, what is Sanatana Dharma or Hinduism all about?
Agreeing on a standard definition of Hinduism is

extremely difficult as it includes such diverse ideas on spirituality developed over centuries. Interestingly, it has no religious authorities, no governing body, no prophet(s) nor any binding holy book. Hindus can choose to be a polytheist, pantheist, monotheist, monist, agnostic, or even an atheist!

It is said that the term Hindu first appeared as a Persian geographical term for the people who lived south of the river Indus (*Sindhu*, in Sanskrit). By that definition, all religious philosophies that evolved within the geographical boundaries of the Indian peninsula could be described as Hinduism. Though that's not the generally accepted definition of Hinduism. Many different religious philosophies originated from the Indian peninsula. They can be largely grouped into two buckets - *Āstika* and *Nāstika*. The *Āstika* philosophies are said to be derived from the *Veda*[1], which is a large body of ancient religious and philosophical texts, and on the other hand, *Nāstika* philosophies[2] are the ones that are not derived from or associated with the *Veda*. Separate from the geographical perspective, it's the philosophies with Vedic foundation (*Āstika*) that are generally accepted as the Hindu philosophies.

In this book, we will be exploring the key ideas contained within the Vedic philosophies or *Āstika*. Note that what we call the Hindu philosophy

---

[1] Veda (Sanskrit: वेद, literal translation - "knowledge") are a large body of religious texts written in Vedic Sanskrit in ancient India. There are four Vedas: the Rigveda, the Yajurveda, the Samaveda and the Atharvaveda.

[2] E.g. Buddhism, Jainism, *Cārvāka*, and *Ājīvika*.

comprises multiple prominent philosophical schools - Sankhya, Yoga, Nyaya, Vaisheshika, Mimamsa and Vedanta. They all treat *Veda* to be the highest authority. Each of these further have multiple sub-schools within them. All of these philosophical schools and sub-schools developed organically over thousands of years through discussions, arguments, contemplation, meditation and experiences have many differences and even contradictions within them which, I say, are healthy signs of living philosophy. This simply adds to the breadth and depth of what we refer to as the Hindu philosophy.

In spite of the diversity contained within Hinduism, as is apparent through the existence of various prominent philosophical schools, there are strong unifying factors as well. Some common themes include *Karma, Dharma, Māyā, Moksha, Kāma, Brahman, Puruṣārtha*, etcetera. In this book, we will go through them all in a way that doesn't only introduce you to these concepts but also explores their relevance in your life.

Does this book comprehensively cover all the different ideas and teachings of the Hindu philosophy?

The short answer to this question is - No. This book attempts to introduce and explore the common and fundamental themes that run across most of the ancient Vedic philosophies (*Āstika*). In particular, this book leans towards the philosophical ideas contained in *Advaita Vedanta*[3].

Of course, Hinduism is not just limited to philosophies but it also has - mythologies and epics and stories that help to bring the philosophical ideas to life; and rituals that followers use in their everyday life to connect with and put in action the philosophical teachings. This book, however, is purely focused on exploring the philosophical ideas contained within Hinduism.

How is this book structured?
This book has been divided into 12 chapters, each one focused on one or two core ideas of the Hindu philosophy. The chapters are in the form of a conversation between 'Aham' and 'Brahman'.

'Aham' or Ego-self (*Ahamkara* in Sanskrit) represents the way we generally perceive ourselves. This is what gives us the feeling of "I" or "mine". It's a feeling of distinctness from others. Our ego tends to create attachments and then build an identity for itself typically on the basis of looks, thoughts, achievements, habits, prejudices, desires, beliefs, passions, possessions, fears and so on. According to the Hindu philosophy of *Advaita Vedanta*, in the process of our spiritual evolution, we move from a dominant Ego-Self to a state where the Ego-Self disappears and we realise our 'true' self - or

---

[3] Advaita Vedanta (/əd.ˈvaɪ.tə vɛdˈantə/ Sanskrit: अद्वैत वेदान्त) is a sub-school within Vedanta. It reflects ideas that emerged from the philosophies contained in the Upanishads, the Brahma Sutras and the Bhagavad Gita.

'*Brahman*'[4], which is a key concept found in the *Veda* and the *Upanishad*. We will learn more about the concept of 'Brahman' later in this book. For now, you can view 'Aham' as a 'seeker' and 'Brahman' as a 'learned guide'.

The conversation between 'Aham' and 'Brahman' will take you through the various key concepts of the Hindu philosophy. In addition, throughout this book, you will find relevant quotations from ancient Hindu scriptures and commentaries by some learned Hindu monks. Please do read through them as they will support the explanation of related concepts.

Note that you will find many italicised Sanskrit and English words in the main body of this book (excludes the sections with quotations from scriptures and monks) that carry a special meaning. Their definitions have generally been discussed in the main body of this book. There is also a glossary section at the end where you can find all the italicised words listed together with their definitions or/and with the location in the book where their meanings can be found.

Why this structure?

This book attempts to explore the teachings of the Hindu philosophy in a way that can resonate with an inquisitive and analytical modern mind. Hence a Q&A structure has been employed, where the seeker

---

[4] Brahman does not refer to the Hindu god Brahma, the Hindu god of creation. Nor does it refer to Brahmin, a class that is a part of the caste system.

('Aham') is unwilling to take anything as gospel and so the seeker asks questions until satisfied. The guide answers these questions drawing from the various teachings of the Hindu philosophy. This forms a logical conversation that ensues between 'Aham' (playing the character of a 'seeker') and 'Brahman' (playing a 'learned guide').

All attempts have been made to explain the reasoning behind the teachings of Hinduism so that you don't have to believe in them as gospel. However, it must also be stated here that relying on logic and analysis may lead to a good 'understanding' but, on its own, it can't help you in 'realising'/'experiencing' the universal truths that the Hindu philosophy teaches. Swami Vivekananda, in his speech at the Parliament of Religions in Chicago, said that "The Hindu religion does not consist in struggles and attempts to believe a certain doctrine or dogma, but in realising - not in believing, but in being and becoming". This realisation and the journey of being/becoming has to be your own - through your own experiences and experiments. On this journey, you will find that conscious and constant curiosity, contemplation and introspection will make your best companions.

One final thing I would like to add here is that the book has a very simplistic writing style, however, the content is fairly dense and concepts are profound. For a better understanding, I strongly recommend going slow and stopping frequently to test the theories and concepts against your own experiences and beliefs. Look out for the texts from ancient scriptures and Hindu monks that are listed in the book and use them to test your thoughts and understanding.

Well, without further ado, let's start with a discussion on one of the fundamental concepts in the Hindu philosophy - Attachments and Desires. In the next chapter, through the conversation between Aham and Brahman, we will explore the meanings of attachments and desires while also discussing their effects on our lives. As per the Hindu philosophy, they are closely related to *Suffering* and *Misery* in one's life. By the way, what do we mean by *Sufferings* and *Miseries*? Let's find the answer in the following chapter.

Hope you enjoy the journey of a seeker...

Chapter 2 - Attachments and Desires

ध्यायतो विषयान्पुंसः सङ्गस्तेषूपजायते |
सङ्गात्सञ्जायते कामः कामात्क्रोधोऽभिजायते ||

क्रोधाद्भवति सम्मोहः सम्मोहात्स्मृतिविभ्रमः |
स्मृतिभ्रंशाद् बुद्धिनाशो बुद्धिनाशात्प्रणश्यति ||

Bhagavad Gita chapter 2 verses 62, 63

By constantly focusing on the objects of the senses, one develops attachment to them. Attachment leads to desire, and desire gives rise to anger (when not satisfied).

Anger leads to clouding of judgment, a state of delusion, which confuses the memory. When the memory is confused, the intellect and understanding fail; and when the intellect and understanding fail, the person is ruined.

'Aham': I surely have many attachments and desires in my life but do they hold any special meaning? How do you describe attachments and desires and how do they affect our lives?

'Brahman': Everyone knows the power of the five senses - Eyes to see; tongue to taste; skin for the sensation of touch; ears to hear; nose to smell; and the ego-mind[5]. You perceive this world with your senses and process it with your ego-mind. Your ego-mind creates a perception of the world with the help of those 5 senses and it also creates a perception of self. Your senses and your mind are very good tools to navigate this world. However, you do not experience this world with equanimity and in a disinterested way. You rather go beyond and use these tools to create likes and dislikes. They become attachments. You can understand attachments as bondages that put a bias in the way you choose to act. Both your likes and dislikes control the way in which you act. They drive your actions towards fulfilling your likes and avoiding your dislikes.

You are attached to numerous things in life such as your self-image, your work, wealth, comforts, name, fame, religion, ideas, philosophies, beliefs, family, friends, your house, your possessions, movies, celebrities, your country, the place where you live, seasons, sports teams, restaurants, specific tastes and cuisines, fragrance, pets, and so on.

Even what you dislike creates attachments that act as bondages for you. Your dislikes influence your *Karma* in the same way as your likes do, albeit in the opposite direction i.e. one will attract and the other will repel. So, both likes and dislikes create attachments or bondages. Note that *Karma* includes three types of actions - kāyik (performed with the body or limbs), vāchik (performed by speaking), and mānasik (performed by the mind - thoughts,

---

[5]Ego-mind denotes a mind driven by the Ego-self. Ego-self has been briefly described in Chapter 1 - Introduction.

analysis, feelings).

From your attachments emanate your desires and then your actions are driven by the motive of fulfilling those desires. For example, your liking for certain tastes will drive you to have certain kinds of food. Similarly, your dislike for physical exercise can drive you away from sports. You choose your actions based on your desires to fulfil your likes and avoid your dislikes. **Eventually, the survival of your peaceful and blissful self becomes dependent on the fulfilment of your desires.**

Senses + Ego-Mind ⇒ Likes + Dislikes ⇒ Attachments ⇒ Desires ⇒ Motive/Intention ⇒ Action/Karma

---

'**Aham**': So, you describe attachments as bondages that dictate our choice of action. That's an interesting way of looking at it. Is that an issue though? Of course, one acts as per his/her likes and dislikes. I can see my likes and dislikes created as per the liking of my senses and what you call my ego-driven mind. It's perhaps easier to recognise the likes and dislikes created by senses but much more complex yet subtle likes and dislikes are created by my mind - such as a liking for certain social status, appreciation and recognition, self-image and so on. Of course, I aspire to fulfil these desires. In fact, because of them, I aspire for better things in life. Do they have an impact on my life that I am not seeing?

'**Brahman**': Sure, you may see a lot of your

attachments to be fairly innocuous and in some cases, beneficial for your life. Let's have a look at the process that you go through when you are driven by your attachments and desires. This will clarify how these attachments and desires are affecting your life.

I have just told you about the chain-reaction that starts from your senses and ego-mind giving rise to likes and dislikes that you become attached to and they turn into desires that drive your actions. Inevitably, when your actions are driven by the motive to fulfil your desires the next step in this chain reaction is *Suffering*.

"If one clings to his attachments, refusing to let go, sorrows will not let go of their grip on him."

-Tirukkural Chapter 35

Let me explain to you how that happens -
Situation 1: Every time you fail to act as per your liking or whenever you are unable to avoid what you dislike, you attract suffering in the form of disappointment, anger, sadness, self-pity, depression, anxiety, shame, discomfort, fear, stress, and so on.
Situation 2: On the other hand, fulfilment of your liking and avoidance of what you dislike can result in pleasure, a sense of pride, excitement, arrogance, greed, inability to let go, and so on.

You will realise that as your actions chase the fulfilment of your desires, you swing between these two sets of situations. The stronger your desires, the wilder the swings. Neither of them is a beneficial state for you, rather both of them amount to *Suffering* and *Misery*. You will find that although your desires will change all through your life, what will remain constant is the *Suffering*. Consider the two situations again, and see if you understand why I am calling both of them as *Suffering* and *Misery*. This *Suffering* or *Misery* is not about the hardships and pains in one's life. Pain and hardship are inevitable, but *Suffering* and *Misery* is your choice. Make sure that you clearly distinguish 'pain and hardship' from '*Suffering* and *Misery*'. Pain and hardship are the undesired situations that life throws at you. You don't have any control over them. However, *Suffering* or *Misery*[6] represents a set of ways in which you mentally or emotionally react to situations in life.

Review the two situations that I have just described, neither of them does you any good. You can apply it to any of your desires, the outcome of chasing your desires will always result in one of the two situations. It's the intensity and nature of your desire that will determine the exact outcome but it will always fall within one of the two sets of situations I explained earlier. Say, you desire obedience from your child - failure to achieve it may cause disappointment or anger while achieving desired obedience will likely

---

[6] Italicised words in the main body of this book, including *Suffering* and *Misery*, carry a specific meaning. The meaning of *Suffering* and *Misery* has been described in the above paragraph and these words have been used throughout this book in italics where they carry exactly the same meaning.

give you a feeling of pride[7] and pleasure. Increasingly stronger desires often lead to greed for more. Doesn't matter which set of outcomes you eventually end up with, it will not result in a <u>lasting</u> calm, peaceful and blissful state.

'Aham': It's interesting to see how you describe *Suffering*. I understand the two situations you describe and the fact that you call both of them - *Suffering*. Even in "Situation 2", where desires are fulfilled has been called *Suffering*, which is so counter-intuitive. I believe you call it so because of the effects it brings with it including arrogance, greed, inability to let go, etcetera. However, aren't you missing out on some other effects as well which can be considered to have a clear positive impact, such as happiness derived from achieving what one desires or its positive effect on one's confidence or the motivation they can generate? And some desires can be truly innocuous such as a desire to watch a movie. Surely these desires have a place in life.

'Brahman': This happiness or pleasure that you are talking about is always ephemeral but I do see what you are trying to say. Moreover, you also say that your desires can drive you to act in positive ways which are good for you. For example, desire to work hard, earn more and have a luxurious life. What could be wrong with that?

'Aham': Correct. That's exactly my point. What's the alternative that you are proposing? Are you trying to

---

[7] Pride may seem like an acceptable feeling to have but its genesis is in the ego.

say that one must not desire anything, as desires inevitably bring *Suffering* and *Misery*? How is that even possible? How can one not have attachments and desires?

'Brahman': Not having attachments is difficult indeed. Desires may seem innocuous as well, however, using them in your life to drive your actions can bring various ill-effects. If you continue to act as per your desires, surely it will cause you to swing between the two sets of outcomes that I explained earlier. If you use them as motivators for yourself then do remember that strong, obsessive desires can cause wilder swings for you when you succeed or fail in satisfying your desires. Alternatively, desires in moderation can help you control or limit those swings to a milder degree. However, irrespective of the degree or intensity of desire, neither of the two sets of resulting outcomes can ever lead you to an eternally calm and blissful state. So why chase temporary or fleeting happiness when eternal bliss is on offer! As we discuss further, you will understand the true meaning of non-attachment, which certainly doesn't mean the absence of zest in life.

'Aham': Well, is an eternally peaceful, calm, blissful state even possible? Does it require renouncing all desires? Without desires, there will be no motives. Not even a motive to work! On what basis will I choose to act, if not to fulfil my desires? Surely there can be good ways of using desires in one's life.

'Brahman': Indeed, an eternally peaceful, calm, blissful state is possible that is free from *Suffering* and *Misery*. We will discuss how it can be experienced.

Now that you have understood what attachments and desires are and how they emanate from likes and dislikes created by the senses and the ego-mind, let's delve deeper and have a look at how desire-driven actions play out in one's life. After that, we can examine if they are at all beneficial or even necessary in one's life.

'Aham': Are you going to tell me a way to suppress the feeling of *Suffering* and *Misery* while enduring the pains and hardships of life?

'Brahman': No, not at all. I am going to show a path where *Sufferings* and *Miseries* are non-existent. Where one need not try to hide one's *Suffering*. Where one need not try to hide one's complaints. The prerequisite for this is the understanding of the genesis of all *Sufferings* and *Miseries* - and they are attachments and desires. When you understand how your attachments and desire drive your life, then you will be better able to appreciate the way out.

दुःखेष्वनुद्विग्नमनाः सुखेषु विगतस्पृहः ।
वीतरागभयक्रोधः स्थितधीर्मुनिरुच्यते ॥

यः सर्वत्रानभिस्नेहस्तत्तत्प्राप्य शुभाशुभम् ।
नाभिनन्दति न द्वेष्टि तस्य प्रज्ञा प्रतिष्ठिता ॥

Bhagavad Gita chapter 2 verse 56, 57

One whose mind remains undisturbed by distress, who does not crave for pleasure, and who is free from attachment, fear, and anger, is the possessor of a steady mind.

One who remains unattached under all conditions, and is neither delighted by good fortune nor dejected by loss, he is a one with perfect knowledge.

Chapter 3 - Karma-Phal (Returns of your Karma)

कर्मण्येवाधिकारस्ते मा फलेषु कदाचन।
मा कर्मफलहेतुर्भूर्मा ते सङ्गोऽस्त्वकर्मणि॥

Bhagavad Gita chapter 2 verse 47

You only have the right to work and perform your duties but not the fruits or rewards thereof. Let not the fruits/rewards of your work be your motivation, and do not be attached to laziness and inaction either.

'Brahman': We were discussing the various desires in one's life and how they drive one to act in order to fulfil those desires. You asked if there is any place for desires in one's life and I said yes, you may have them but it will never let you reach an eternally blissful state devoid of *Suffering*. Let me tell you about some popular desires and their resulting pursuits in life.

In Hinduism, four goals or aims of human life have been defined - Puruṣārtha (Sanskrit: पुरुषार्थ) means an "object of human pursuit". They are - Kāma (pleasure of various kinds including love and sexual desire), Artha (primarily means economic prosperity), Dharma (vaguely refers to righteousness/ moral values but has other connotations as well) and Moksha (liberation)[8].

---

[8] There are no direct translations of these words - *Dharma, Artha, Kāma* and *Moksha* - in English. The definition of *Artha* and *Kama* have been shared in this chapter but we will discuss the concepts of *Dharma* and *Moksha* later in the book.

One can pursue Artha and Kāma but they shouldn't be pursued at the expense of or in violation of Dharma. Above all other pursuits, Moksha is considered the ultimate ideal of human life.

There are various things that you may desire in life. Most of your desires could be clubbed under two popular pursuits - Pleasure or *Kāma*, in Sanskrit, and Prosperity or *Artha*, in Sanskrit.

Kāma denotes all kinds of pleasures in life including the pleasure of the senses, aesthetic pleasures such as arts, dance, music, painting, sculpture and nature, emotional attraction, affection, sexual and erotic pleasures, etcetera.

Artha implies "means of life" or resources that enable one to be in a state one wants to be in. This includes wealth, career, financial security, health, economic prosperity, etcetera. Just like *Kāma, Artha* is also an acceptable and important pursuit of life. Thus, desires leading to these pursuits are also acceptable.

In spite of being perfectly acceptable pursuits, your attachment to these desires and their pursuits can still trigger a chain of *Suffering* for you.

'Aham': So, it seems that most of the popular desires that people have and their pursuit in life are acceptable from what you just explained. Isn't it? So why this *Suffering*? What goes wrong if one works for the rewards or the returns it promises? Why can't I achieve a lasting peaceful and blissful state devoid of any *Suffering* when I pursue those desires? Yes, there may be some ill-effects but overall, I believe that they bring positive outcomes and improvements in life.

Take the case of my work life, I see countless examples where careful use of incentives and disincentives can help achieve better results. Shouldn't I aspire for rewards such as bigger performance bonus, early promotion, awards? How else will I motivate myself for bigger challenges if not for bigger rewards?

'Brahman': You are right about the way incentives have been laid out for you in life. That's how the systems around you have been designed and understandably so because that's what you have been responding to. Why do those incentives motivate you?

'Aham': Well, that's what I aspire for. It's a measure of my success.

'Brahman': Isn't completing your task with perfection a success in itself?

'Aham': Yes, it is but why lose out on the benefits and rewards?

'Brahman': No, you don't need to lose out on the benefits but you do have to distinguish between being motivated by or driven by the work alone and being driven by the returns from the work. Many times, it's not a case of either/or but a mix of motivations that drive your actions.

Understanding the impact of desires driving your actions is so critical that I am explaining it again. Each of the motivators behind your work or act has its own impact. If you are attached to or are motivated by the returns or rewards from your work, such as name, fame, bonus, position, recognition and so on, both the success as well the failure of achieving those rewards/returns will bring you *Sufferings* that come in the form of -

[set 1] - when you fail to get the desired rewards for your work - disappointment, stress, sadness, anxiety, shame, sadness, under-confidence, self-criticism; and also

[set 2] - when you get the desired rewards for your work - pride, pleasure, greed, excitement, overconfidence, arrogance and so on.

As we discussed earlier, both the sets amount to *Suffering*, although, you naively aspire to resist only the former set.

Remember they are simply two sides of the same coin. One can't exist without the other. If you think about it long and hard, you will realise that none of those two sets actually make your life any better. The world around you works in such a way that you can never escape this endless cycle of *Suffering*. I call it endless because the pleasure you are seeking in this mode of work is ephemeral, fleeting, transient... your chase never ends and you keep swinging between the two sets of *Sufferings* that we have discussed.

---

sukhāya karmāṇi karoti loko na taiḥ sukhaṁ vānyad-upāramaṁ vā

vindeta bhūyas tata eva duḥkhaṁ yad atra yuktaṁ bhagavān vaden naḥ

Srimad-Bhagavatam Part 3 Chapter 5 Verse 2
Commentary by Swami Mukundananda

"Every human being engages in fruitive[9] works to get happiness, but finds no satisfaction. Instead, these activities only aggravate the misery."

As a result, practically everyone in this world is unhappy. Some suffer from the miseries of their own body and mind; others are tormented by their family members and relatives; some suffer from scarcity of wealth and the paucity of the necessities of life.

Materially minded people know they are unhappy, but they think that others ahead of them must be happy, and so they continue running in the direction of material growth. This blind pursuit has been going on for many lifetimes and yet there is no sight of happiness. Now, if people could realise that nobody has ever achieved happiness by engaging in fruitive works, they would then understand that the direction in which they are running is futile.

Needless to say, that expectation of returns from your work can distract your focus from the work itself. **You will often find that when driven by the returns of the work, your mind will be fixated on the returns that you desire instead of the work at hand.** In such a case, it is not helping you as you approach work with an unfocused or distracted mind. You will

---

[9] Fruit-bearing or returns that fulfil personal desires.

27

see numerous such cases in real life when all one cares about is the desire or reward that he/she is chasing and, on the way, the work itself gets compromised. **The intensity of desired rewards/returns sometimes becomes so strong that the work itself becomes irrelevant and the person is willing to do anything to satisfy one's desires**. That's why I say, be very careful about what you desire and be very conscious of the intensity of your desires.

'Aham': You are saying that attachment with returns associated with the work or being motivated by them creates distractions and brings *Suffering* for us. However, these rewards are important in one's life. As you say, they may be the desire of pleasure (*Kāma*) and prosperity (*Artha*) but they have some very practical benefits as well, for example - with the money my life could be more comfortable, with a higher position I can take on greater responsibilities and so on. This desire of reward could be a good motivator!

'Brahman': No denying the fact that you may receive certain returns or rewards to your work/action that can be beneficial to your life in some ways. It's the expectation and attachment with the returns of your work that is the distraction and the cause of *Suffering*. Study your own past experiences and you will realise that **you only have control over the work you do or the effort you put in but not on the returns you can get from it**. So, what you should aspire for is to treat whatever return comes to you with equanimity. If you learn to approach all actions in that way then there will be no *Suffering* for you.

Many also feel that the expectation of rewards/returns is the ultimate motivator to do the work in the best possible manner. Thus, it helps to perform better. This argument of using desire to improve your work is extremely dangerous. It simply pushes you into the never-ending cycle of *Suffering* where you are left forever chasing illusory happiness and it rather keeps you from attaining an eternally peaceful and blissful state. So why should one settle for *Suffering* instead of eternal calm and bliss? Though the choice is still yours. Also, I will show you that achieving excellence or doing your best need not be dependent on the Returns/Rewards of the work. You can achieve excellence and also get rid of all *Sufferings* and *Miseries* at the same time.

'**Aham**': So, in that case, what will motivate me to improve and excel? Also, please tell me how can I act in a way that doesn't bring *Suffering*? What's the alternative that can help me break this cycle of *Suffering* and *Misery*?

'**Brahman**': The answer is *Nishkāma Karma* and detachment. You can't escape *Karma* i.e. you cannot exist without engaging in one or the other form of *Karma* - either physical or mental. Remember that emotions or feelings are also simply the result of the physical and the mental acts coming together. So, you always have to act but you will have to do so without an expectation of returns thereof. The only way is *Nishkāma Karma* and detachment.

'**Aham**': And what is *Nishkāma Karma*?

Chapter 4 - Nishkāma Karma

'Aham': What is *Nishkāma Karma*?

'Brahman': *Nishkāma Karma* means desire-less actions or actions that are not performed for self-benefits. It means selfless actions without even a subtle hope for niceties being returned. No desire for rewards, recognitions, favours or even a promise of heaven.

The only way of avoiding any and all forms of *Suffering* that inevitably comes along with every *Karma* is to work for the sake of work alone, as the means is also the end. When you have no attachments and desires driving your actions then there is no associated *Suffering*.

'Aham': This is sounding impractical and unrealistic. Is it even possible to work without some kind of selfish motive? Is it the case of altruism which doesn't even exist because one derives happiness and pride from the good work that one does? These are not external rewards but very basic desires that drive every human being.

'Brahman': Practical is what seems doable within the environment that exists around you. So, I am not surprised if *Nishkāma Karma* sounds alien in this environment. *Nishkāma Karma*, however, is not impossible or even impractical.

You talk of deriving happiness and pride from altruistic activities. Well, helping others is good but helping others without a sense of pride or greatness is even better. One who helps someone and instantly puts oneself at a higher pedestal, and it happens very often, thinking that he/she has done something great is actually foolish. **This feeling of pride and greatness about yourself is the work of your ego-mind**. It's only your ego-mind that derives satisfaction from such thinking. So, altruism in its truest sense is possible once you have ridden yourself of your ego. That's the only hindrance.

Irrespective of the work you are undertaking, whether you are helping someone or shooting a target or solving a complex mathematical problem or writing prose or doing anything else, trying to do it as well as possible is all that you need to care about. If you have done it well, move to your next action. In the process, try to improve yourself at doing what you do. However, feeling proud and deriving a sense of achievement from it is purely ego-driven. If you stay driven by the desire to please your ego then the *Sufferings* in life will never end for you. Arjuna and Krishna[10] are great examples, where Arjuna was full of pride because of his unmatched skills as a warrior but Krishna was never proud of himself even though he was the greatest in every respect.

तस्मादसक्तः सततं कार्यं कर्म समाचर |
असक्तो ह्याचरन्कर्म परमाप्नोति पूरुषः ||

Bhagavad Gita chapter 3 verse 19

---

[10] As per the epic *Mahābhārata*, Arjuna was considered the greatest archer. Krishna is an incarnation of Lord Vishnu.

Therefore, giving up attachment, diligently perform actions as a matter of duty, working without being attached to the fruits/returns from the work, one attains the Supreme.

'Aham': Just as you were saying earlier, the work of our ego-driven mind leads us to the set of *Sufferings* that include the feeling of pride, greatness, arrogance, pleasure and so on. You say that these drivers are not necessary at all. Well, I still don't understand how one can practice detachment - not driven by likes and dislikes, not driven by attachment and desires. And if I am detached from my work then why would I even be bothered about the result of my actions or say the quality of my work?

'Brahman': Detachment is often misunderstood and, in many cases, not understood at all. When it is said that you are attached to your work what does it really mean? In the context of *Suffering* caused by attachments, it is said that you are attached to your work when you desire something in return for the work. This could be recognition, appreciation, favours, reward or, in the purest sense, even the pleasure you derive from the work itself[11]!

As you work as per your attachments and desires, the *Law of Karma* ensures that your attachments and desires get even more entrenched in your character or nature, making it even more difficult for you to

---

[11] This topic has been further discussed in the chapter on Duty.

escape the *Sufferings* of life.

I will tell you more about the *Law of Karma* later and let me first answer your question about the quality of work delivered and the sincerity that is required to do the work well.

Detachment doesn't mean being indifferent towards the work being done. Think of it like a nurse who cares for and fondles and plays with your baby as if the baby was her own child, but as soon as her job is done, she is ready to leave and she gets ready to attend to another child. Thus, she remains fully absorbed in her work but still unattached. Leaving the child doesn't create any pain or pleasure for her[12].

So, distinguish between 'Result' and 'Returns'. Practising conscientiousness in one's actions is paramount. Remember the episode from the epic *Mahābhārata*[13] when *Guru*[14] Dronacharya asked the *Kauravas* and *Pandavas*[15] to aim at a wooden bird hanging from a tree. Arjuna, the greatest archer, was the only one who could focus on the bird's eye and was successfully able to hit the target. Hence, intense focus on your target to successfully complete the

---

[12] Adapted from the teachings of Sri Ramakrishna Paramhansa.

[13] The *Mahābhārata* is an epic that narrates the struggle between two groups of cousins - the Kaurava and the Pāṇḍava princes. It's marked by the famous battle of *Kurukshetra* and the revered Bhagavad Gita.

[14] Teacher.

[15] Kauravas and Pandavas are the warrior princes from the epic *Mahābhārata*.

33

work at hand is non-negotiable. However, **the expectation of returns or being driven by returns of your work is inessential for achieving perfection in one's work**.

Rather attachment with the returns of your work simply disturbs your focus on the work itself and introduces biases in your thoughts and actions. We have already discussed[16] how an intense attachment with returns/rewards can even cause the work to be compromised if it helps to achieve the desired returns! Such behaviours are often visible in people who are willing to cut corners and even indulge in wrong-doings to accumulate, say wealth/power, at all cost. Work in itself becomes immaterial for them as all they care about is to anyhow fulfil those desires.

We must love God for love's sake, so we must do our duty for duty's sake; we must work for work's sake without looking for any reward — know that you are purer and more perfect, know that this is the real temple of God."
- Swami Vivekananda, Brooklyn Daily Eagle, December 31, 1894

'Aham': I can see how my attachments can introduce bias in the way I undertake my work. You say that if I want to avoid *Suffering,* I must work without selfish desires. You are suggesting me to work with a sense of duty just the way a nurse does her duty without getting attached to the work itself but still provides the best possible care. That's the way to achieve excellence without the need for any kind of

---

[16] Discussed in the chapter on *Karma-Phal.*

attachments. Honestly, I still have more questions about it but please first explain to me the *Law of Karma*. You talked about it earlier and indicated that it causes attachments and desires to get entrenched in one's character and thus influences all future actions. Do you mean this cycle of attachment → desire → motive → action → *Suffering* is a reinforcing cycle that grows stronger with time? Is that what the *Law of Karma* says?

After that, please also explain to me on what basis do I choose my actions, if not on the basis of my desires? A nurse may be acting purely in order to serve the patients or a teacher may be acting purely in order to share his/her knowledge. These acts may be completely free of selfish-desires but still, there is a desire. A desire to serve or a desire to teach. Are these acceptable desires and are the duties or actions emanating from such selfless desires acceptable?

'Brahman': Ok, let me first explain to you the *Law of Karma* and then we will come back to your question about the basis of choosing one's actions when we discuss the concept of duty.

Chapter 5 - Law of Karma

'Aham': What is the *Law of Karma*?

'Brahman': The *Law of Karma*, also known as the law of causation, is a universal law which simply means every action will have a commensurate effect. This *cause* and *effect* phenomenon cannot be avoided[17].

Anything that you do or think or feel has an effect on you. Consider the basic parts of a sentence that you study in grammar - Subject, Verb, Object[18]. Your *karma*/actions ('Verb') will have a corresponding effect or impact on the 'Object' of the verb as well as on the 'Subject'. Discerning the effect of your action on the 'Object' of the 'Verb' or the object of your action is often far simpler than discerning its effect on the 'Subject' itself, in other words, on your own self. When discussing the *Law of Karma*, we are less interested in the impact of your action on the 'object' and more interested in the impact of your action on the subject i.e. yourself.

Of course, your action will have its impact on the person or thing that your action is directed towards, but what's the impact of your *Karma* on your own self?

Your *Karma* is making an impact on you all the time,

[17] This is not related to action and reaction associated with Newton's third law of motion!

[18] In the sentence 'I advised Neil', I is the subject, advised is the verb and Neil is the object.

and the impact it makes on you is determined by your intent or motive behind your actions. That is why motive or intent becomes so critical.

Both the (1) type of impact and the (2) degree of impact your karma has on you is driven by your motive behind the *karma*. In other words, it's not the action itself that you perform but the intention with which you performed it creates the impact that you accumulate for yourself. Over time, you thus accumulate a lot of impact on yourself!

Man consists of desires,
As his desire is, so is his determination,
As his determination is, so is his deed,
Whatever his deed is, that he attains.
— Brihadaranyaka Upanishad

For example, a doctor carrying out a record number of treatments on a daily basis could be doing it with different motives. The motive could be to earn a lot of money as one gets paid for every treatment carried out, or the motive could be to get award and recognition for the treatments performed, or the doctor might simply be acting with a sense of duty and so on; or a combination of these motives. You will see that the *Karma* in all these cases is the same - treating the patients. However, the impact of the same *Karma* on the doctor will be different in each case depending upon the specific motives behind the action.

Let me explain the effects of *Karma* on one's own self. We use the word *Karma* in many different ways and one of them is to mean that your *Karma* comes back to you in the form of a *Karmic Cycle*. But 'what' is it that comes back? In the case of the doctor performing a record number of treatments, it doesn't mean the doctor will necessarily get treatment when he needs one, just because he has performed several treatments for others. It isn't the treatments that he has accumulated for himself but he is really amassing the motives/intentions with which he has performed the treatments. If it was the greed for money with which the doctor treated his patients then it's that greed that the doctor has accumulated for himself. As the actions and the motives get repeated over time, they make a distinct mark on one's character or nature. As the character gets shaped by the motives so do the future actions. This is the guaranteed effect of the motives behind one's actions. These motives reinforced in one's character will then have an even greater tendency to influence future actions of the person. This is how the *Law of Karma* works - attachments and desires create selfish motives/intentions that drive one's actions and, in the process, further strengthens those desires and motives influencing future actions as well.

Senses + Ego-Mind ⇒ Likes + Dislikes ⇒ Attachments ⇒ Desires ⇒ Motive/Intention ⇒ Action/Karma

Let's take another example, say of a pickpocket, to get a clearer understanding of the effects of one's *Karma*. The *Law of Karma* doesn't ensure that a pickpocket will one day get his own wallet stolen. However, the *Law of Karma* guarantees that over time, his motive behind stealing will further impact his character and drive his future actions. Say, if it was greed that made him steal then his repeated acts of stealing will make greed an even more prominent part of his nature/character. This is why selfish motives and intentions behind one's *Karma* are said to create binding effects i.e. motives/intentions behind one's *Karma* create deeper bondages that drive future *Karma* as well. His increasingly greed-driven actions can manifest in different ways in his life. His greed could drive him to take greater risks for a bigger steal eventually leading him to a day when his luck runs out. Or in another instance, his increasingly greedy character may even affect his private relationships turning them sour over time.

'Aham': You are saying that two persons engaging in exactly the same act or *Karma* but with different motives will be impacted differently depending on their motives.

'Brahman': Yes, and it doesn't stop there as it triggers a chain reaction that further fuels the cycle. Deep attachments and desires creating motives that result in a deeper impact on your nature or character further controlling your future actions. Thus creating a never-ending cycle. This is also described as the binding effects of your *Karma* that keeps you entangled in the endless cycle of your actions and the consequences of those actions on yourself.

The way out of this is to work without any desires originating from one's likes/dislikes or attachments. Work with a sense of duty or sacrifice or work for the sake of work alone. For the doctor, carrying out all the treatments purely with a sense of duty will relieve him of motives that can fuel the *Karmic Cycle* thus freeing him from any bondage created by his *Karma* and thus freeing him from the related *Sufferings*.

यज्ञार्थात्कर्मणोऽन्यत्र लोकोऽयं कर्मबन्धनः |
तदर्थं कर्म कौन्तेय मुक्तसङ्गः समाचर ||

Bhagavad Gita chapter 3 verse 9

Work must be done as a yajña (sacrifice); otherwise, work causes bondage in this material world. Therefore, O son of Kunti, work only for the sake of work, without being attached to the work or the returns thereof.

'Aham': So, working with a sense of duty or sacrifice or for the sake of work alone can relieve me from the binding effects of my *Karma*. But how is it that the *karma* itself has no role to play but the motive or the intention that determines the binding effect of my *Karma*? Surely there are good and evil deeds that will have an impact on the doer.

'Brahman': Ok let me first tell you about good and evil. Then we will get back to the discussion on what can drive your actions, if not your selfish desires.

Chapter 6 - Good and Evil

'Brahman': What is a good deed and what is an evil deed? This is a complex question. You would often judge good or bad by the moral standards set by the society you live in. These moral standards are a reflection of a complex mix of various attributes such as the day and age, the culture, the value system, the beliefs, local history, and so on. We need not debate here the moral standards set by different societies. Definition of morality changes with time and place. You can define good and evil as per one moral system prevalent in one country or society and it will have conflicting interpretations under another moral system in another country or society.

More importantly, if you scrutinise any piece of work you will find that none is perfectly holy or perfectly evil. Say a hungry man came to your doorstep and you fed him some food. This seems like a good deed but you forget that to feed him you took the life of a plant or an animal. The war in *Kurukshetra*[19] ended after numerous lives were lost and it established the rule of the *Pandavas*. Can you call them purely holy acts? Your very life on this earth is crowding out other lives! How can one ever imagine to not engage in what is generally considered evil?

"We read in the Bhagavad Gita again and again that we must all work incessantly. All work is by nature

---

[19] Kurukshetra is the place where the final war described in the Hindu epic *Mahābhārata* was fought.

composed of good and evil. We cannot do any work which will not do some good somewhere; there cannot be any work which will not cause some harm somewhere. Every work must necessarily be a mixture of good and evil; yet we are commanded to work incessantly."

- *Swami Vivekananda - The Secret of Work*

If you do believe in the concept of sin, evil, good, virtuosity then you will find that it is impossible to have an act that is purely holy or purely evil. You will find all work to be a mix of some good elements and some evil elements which is determined by the perspective or the lens you use to assess that work.

So, let me tell you that **what you call 'sin' is not in the action itself but in your motive or intention behind the act**. There is no inherently good or bad action/*Karma*, rather actions in itself are neutral. A doctor and an assassin may both inflict pain on you but the intention will be very different and the intention will dictate what is good and what is evil. Your motive, which is so often driven by your attachments and desires, makes a deed good or bad.

Moreover, if your acts are driven by selfish intentions of gratifying your senses and ego then you will be bound by the effects of your *Karma* as we had discussed earlier when we talked about the *Law of Karma*.

Let's take another example. You will definitely consider robbery an evil act. In contrast, how would you describe a government levying taxes? If the government levy taxes not for the larger public good but for the benefit of a select few then would it be any different from robbery? Perhaps, not. So again, your concern should be the intention or motive behind one's act.

'Aham': But what if I act thinking that it's for the good of others however, in effect, it may not end up helping others? In that case, even if I act without any selfish motive, still my actions may harm others. For example, parents may force their views on their children assuming that they know what is right for their kids or a person like Robinhood may rob the rich to serve the poor. In these cases, despite selfless intentions, the kids may be unduly subjugated or some of the rich may have to face unjustified instances of robbery. How will these actions be judged and how are the actors impacted?

'Brahman': All your *Karma* create two kinds of impact - (1) an impact on yourself through your motive/intention as I explained in our discussion on the *Law of Karma*; and (2) an impact on the person or thing that your action was directed towards[20].

Say, you are absolutely selflessly advising your son. Your act of advising is in no way driven by peer pressure, desire to gain respect in society or even the expectation of support in your old age. With non-attachment and *Nishkāma Karma* you may escape the impact # 1 - i.e. binding effects of *Karma* on yourself, however, you still have to face the impact # 2 - i.e. impact of your action on your son and his

---

[20] In some cases, your action could be directed towards your own self such as learning a new skill.

response to it. This is the 'Return' (*Karma-Phal*) of your *Karma* on which you have no control[21].

Your skills as an advisor will have a role to play in the impact that your advice creates on your son. However, the response of your child will be driven by his own character that is shaped by his desires and attachments. Your son may find your advice suffocating and choose to rebel or, alternatively, might find value in your advice and implement it in his life. That's something that you will still have to face and you won't have control over what comes to you in 'return' of your actions irrespective of what your intentions were.

You should be interested in being acutely aware of yourself and notice if the urge to advise and influence your child is purely selfless. Your well-intentioned advice, in reality, could have slipped into the desire of seeing yourself in your child or the desire to satisfy your desires through your child! This can reflect a very different motive and bring upon a different set of consequences for you as per the *Law of Karma*. Remember that your motives and desires will stick with you and influence your future actions. Hence aspire for *Nishkāma Karma* - desireless actions performed with conscientiousness and a sense of duty[22]. You need not bother about anything else. Don't be bogged down by the thought of judging all acts. You don't need to. *Nishkāma Karma* will ensure that there are no binding effects of your *Karma*.

---

[21] No rights to the returns of your *Karma* as discussed in the chapter on *Karma-Phal*.

[22] The word duty here doesn't mean an obligation. This has been further discussed in the chapter on Duty.

ब्रह्मण्याधाय कर्माणि सङ्गं त्यक्त्वा करोति यः |
लिप्यते न स पापेन पद्मपत्रमिवाम्भसा ||

Bhagavad Gita chapter 5 verse 10

*Those who dedicate their actions to the Brahman,
abandoning all attachments, remain untouched by sin,
just as a lotus leaf is untouched by water.*

'Aham': I think I understand what you mean when
you say to focus on the motive and the spirit with
which the work is done. You also say that one can
transcend the binding effects of *Karma* by engaging
in *Nishkāma Karma*. For this, we need to work with
a sense of duty or work for the sake of work alone.
What does that mean? What does this sense of duty
or sacrifice or work for the sake of work mean? And,
what are my duties? Is there any prescribed set of
acts or duties that one should always undertake?

Chapter 7 - Duty

'Aham': So often you have talked about acting with a sense of duty. Please explain to me what do you mean by working with a sense of duty or working for the sake of work alone? And, what is my duty?

'Brahman': Let me first explain to you what is meant when I say - work with a sense of duty or work for the sake of work alone. Later on, we will discuss what could constitute one's duties.

When I talk about working with a sense of duty it definitely doesn't mean working as an obligation. The spirit with which you work is of prime importance here. Earlier when we discussed *Nishkāma Karma*, I had given you an example of a nurse to elaborate on what it means to work with a sense of duty. No matter what you do, that's the spirit with which you need to act. The spirit to do the job as good as you can but without any attachment[23] or expectation of returns or rewards thereof. Not even an attachment with the work itself or the output of your work. No scope for pride or shame. **Focus purely on the job at hand, finish it, consciously learn from your experience to improve in future and move on.** Let me give you another example of a painter. As a painter, just focus on the work at hand i.e. painting, make the best painting you can, consciously correct your mistakes and make improvements, and after you have painted your masterpiece, move to your next

---

[23] Refer to chapter on attachment and desire. Attachments emanate from your likes and dislikes that are created by the ego-mind and the five senses. There could be an attachment to the returns of your *Karma* and even with the *Karma* itself. All attachments must be renounced.

painting. There need not be any attachment with the painting itself, even if it is the most beautiful piece you have ever painted. If you lose it for some reason there is no pain. You have moved on already. That's the spirit with which you need to work. Work for the sake of that work alone and not for the returns thereof. Don't even get attached to your work. Approach all work with equanimity, with neither affinity nor aversion. Keep your focus on performing the work as well as possible and, of course, avoid inaction. This is the spirit with which I am asking you to work and it will relieve you from all *Sufferings* and also guide you towards excellence.

बुद्धियुक्तो जहातीह उभे सुकृतदुष्कृते ।
तस्माद्योगाय युज्यस्व योगः कर्मसु कौशलम् ॥

Bhagavad Gita chapter 2 verse 50

A wise person works without attachments and can get rid of both virtue and vice in this life itself. Therefore, strive for Yoga (union of Aham and Brahman), which is the art of <u>working with the highest skill</u>.

'Aham': I think I understand what you mean when you say working with a sense of duty or working for the sake of work alone and the example of how a nurse works, makes it even clearer to me. However, how do I choose my work or my duty? Or in fact, how do I choose my actions if it is not driven by my desires? What's my duty? Without this knowledge, I will sit idle as I have nothing to accomplish, nothing to chase, nothing to fulfil. But you say, I must also avoid inaction. How is it possible?

'Brahman': You have many queries troubling you at the moment. Let's first focus on this question - what should one pursue in life?

I had briefly touched upon the topic of various pursuits in one's life during our conversation on *Karma-Phal*. You can pursue *Kāma* and *Artha* but if your actions are driven by those pursuits, they will create binding effects as per the *Law of Karma*. Note that they are still acceptable pursuits of life as long as they are not pursued at the expense of *Dharma*. I will explain the concept of *Dharma* in a moment. Remember though that pursuit of *Kāma* and *Artha* will not free you from the binding effects of your *Karma* and thus will not free you from the *Sufferings* and *Miseries* of life.

There is a way to rise above selfish motives and undertake selfless acts for the larger good of society/world. Let me now tell you about *Dharma*[24]. *Dharma* signifies behaviours that are considered to be in accordance with rta[25], the order that allows the whole universe to function in harmony. It is often understood as moral correctness, universal law, universal truth and righteousness. **Following Dharma is different for each person, meaning that everyone has a particular role or duty which one has to discover and uphold.** *Dharma*, as individuals live in harmony with one another and oneself, keeps the universe in balance. We call our own *Dharma* or our

---

[24] *Dharma* is derived from root *Dhr* meaning 'to hold'. Activities/Actions which contribute in holding the society/world in harmony are acts of *Dharma*.

[25] Ṛta (/ˈr̩tə/; Sanskrit ऋत "order; rule; truth") is the truth or the principle of the natural order which regulates and coordinates the operation of the universe and everything within it.

own path of duty as - *Swadharma.*

Note that there are many connotations of the word *Dharma* but it definitely doesn't mean religion in any case.

If I have to state it simply, I will say that when you act selflessly to keep the world functioning in harmony, you are undertaking acts of *Dharma* - e.g. teaching your students (teacher), treating your patients (doctor), enabling a market where goods and services could be exchanged (trader), physically arranging necessary goods for the world to function (logistics provider), conducting research in the areas of various sciences (scientist), helping maintain order and safety (police, military), keeping the world clean (sanitation worker), feeding the world (farmer), ensuring the safety and security of a family (head of family), learning new work skills (student) and so on. All of them are acceptable acts of *Dharma.* Do it with selfless motive. Remember from our earlier conversations about *Karma* that it's the motive or intention behind your *Karma* that makes all the difference.

'Aham': But all these acts of *Dharma*, which ultimately benefit the larger society or the world, could also be carried out for other motives such as for creating wealth or gaining appreciation, praise, position, etc. Isn't it?

'Brahman': True. All the jobs/work I have just stated fall within the acts of *Dharma.* One can pursue them purely for the sake of *Dharma,* in other words, purely for supporting the harmonious functioning of the society or the world. Alternatively, one can also choose to undertake these acts with the intention of fulfilling one's desires for *Kāma* and/or *Artha*. As I said earlier, chasing *Kāma* and Artha will still be acceptable pursuits as long as they are in accordance with *Dharma*. The obvious downside is that when you act with the desire for *Kāma* or *Artha*, your motives will create binding effects on you as per the *Law of Karma*. Moreover, all such desires create distractions from the job itself as there is a tendency for your focus to shift from the work itself to the returns you will get from your work. These are topics that we have already discussed when we talked about *Karma-Phal* and *Nishkāma Karma*.

'Aham': And can one act in a way that is not in accordance with *Dharma*? I reckon those will be unacceptable pursuits though.

'Brahman': Yes, there are so many such cases. These are called acts of *Adharma,* in other words, acts that are not in accordance with *Dharma.* Such acts of *Adharma* include *Karma* that creates disharmony, discord, hate, pain in the world. For example, when a doctor is treating patients purely for the pursuit of money then that pursuit is still an <u>acceptable</u> pursuit as the act itself is in accordance with *Dharma*, i.e. treating patients, even though the motive behind the work is purely *Artha* (economic prosperity, wealth). However, if an impersonator is pretending to be a doctor and defrauding his/her patients to earn money, then this pursuit of *Artha* is unacceptable as the person is engaging in acts of *Adharma*,

50

mistreating people and society[26].

'Aham': I think I understand why you call *Adharma* unacceptable. However, distinguishing between the acts of Dharma and Adharma can sometimes be tricky. I have more questions in that regard. However, before I seek your help there, I have another intriguing observation to clarify. You just highlighted so many different jobs involved in keeping the world functioning in harmony as per the definition of *Dharma*, such as that of a teacher, a doctor, a scientist, a farmer and so on. You put all of them on the same pedestal. That's surprising. Are there no distinctions between the various acts that are performed in accordance with *Dharma*?

'Brahman': It may look surprising to you but that is correct. Societies and individuals may judge professions on the basis of hardship entailed, rewards associated, position of power and authority and so on. However, from a spiritual perspective, there are no distinctions. Irrespective of one's profession or work, as long as they are in accordance with *Dharma*, everyone can aspire for freedom from the *Karmic Cycle* and S*uffering*.

Let me tell you a popular, ancient story. Once a monk was asked to go to Mithila[27] to meet a Vyādha, a community of people in India who used to live as

---

[26] Do remember though that *Dharma* and *Adharma* do not mean 'Religious' and 'Irreligious'. As clarified earlier, *Dharma* doesn't translate to Religion.

[27] A region located in the Indian state of Bihar.

hunters, to learn an important lesson on spirituality and *Dharma*. The monk went to meet the Vyādha and saw him cutting meat with big knives, talking and bargaining with different people. The monk said to himself, "Lord help me! Is this the man from whom I am going to learn? He is the incarnation of a demon, if he is anything." The Vyādha man went on with his work. After finishing his job, he took the monk home. On reaching home the Vyadha gave him a seat, saying, "Wait here" and he went into the house. He then fed his parents and did all he could to please them, after which he came to the monk and said, "Sir, you have come here to see me; what can I do for you?" The monk asked him a few questions about soul and God, and the Vyādha gave him a lecture which forms a part of the *Mahābhārata*, called the Vyādha-Gitā. When the Vyādha finished his teaching, the monk felt astonished. He said, "With such knowledge as yours why are you in a Vyādha's body, and doing such filthy, ugly work?" "My son," replied the Vyādha, "no duty is ugly, no duty is impure. My birth placed me in these circumstances and environments. When I was young, I learnt the trade; I am unattached, and I try to do my duty well. I try to do my duty as a householder, and I try to do all I can to make my father and mother happy. I neither know your Yoga, nor have I become a monk, nor did I go out of the world into a forest; nevertheless, all that you have heard and seen has come to me through unattached performance of the duty which belongs to my position."

He who does the lower work (supposedly) is not, therefore, a lower man. No man is to be judged by the *mere nature of his duties, but all should be judged by the manner and the spirit in which they perform them.*

The householder by digging tanks, by planting trees on the roadsides, by establishing rest-houses for men and animals, by making roads and building bridges, goes towards the same goal as the greatest Yogi.
- *Swami Vivekananda on - social/professional duties and Karma*

Circumstances and life choices can put you in certain social and professional situations. In that context, your duty is to work to the best of your ability and with detachment[28]. Your duties are not impediments to your freedom from *Sufferings* as long as they are performed without selfish motives.

'Aham': Ok, I understand that. Though you only talk about professional duties. Is that all there is?

'Brahman': Oh no. Societies are an integral part of this world. Social context is a key driver behind deciding one's duties. Generally, you will be acting within the social realms of the society that you live in. Societies decide a lot of duties and moralities for their members. Though, be aware that the moralities and duties may differ in different societies and in different times. Also, duties change with the stage of life. Your duties as a young student will not be the same as that of an adult leading a family. You could see how the Vyādha, in the ancient story I shared earlier, meticulously performed his professional

---

[28] This was discussed earlier in the chapter on *Nishkāma Karma*.

duties as well as the duty towards his parents emanating from his position of being a son as defined in the social context.

In relation to social duties, do remember that the social duties and moralities prescribed in one society may be seen as a sin in another society or another age.

Therefore, the one point we ought to remember is that we should always try to see the duty of others through their own eyes, and never judge the customs of other people by our own standards. I am not the standard of the universe. I have to accommodate myself to the world, and not the world to me. So we see that environments change the nature of our duties, and doing the duty which is ours at any particular time is the best thing we can do in this world.

- *Swami Vivekananda on "What is Duty"*

Even in a relatively homogenous society, sometimes, it becomes difficult to define and agree on a common definition of social responsibilities and duties. It is always advisable to pursue mutual consensus between all relevant stakeholders. Mere differences in views do not make them wrong or unacceptable. In such situations anchor your analysis on the intention behind the action. If intentions are selfish or ego-driven then it's worth avoiding. Intentions, again, are paramount in making the correct choice.

Also, beware that yours and your society's moral systems may get corrupted at times. While it may be prudent to be aware and consistent with such moral systems but don't take them to be perfect. If you go through the history of this world, time and again, you would see instances of imperfection in human society. On many occasions, you will find widely held beliefs in masses that have proven to be harmful to mankind rather than beneficial. Sometimes, certain moral standards are only suitable for a specific time or under specific circumstances. However, so often we find them causing more harm than good when they outlive their utility but societies continue to abide by them even after they have become irrelevant. It typically happens as people become dependent on habits, they get attached to set ways of living and then their awareness drops. On other occasions, societies and individuals sometimes pick up virtues that are outright selfish and not in the interest of humanity. Such virtues are often driven by the objective of satisfying their collective ego. Honour killing is one very relevant example where collective ego can drive the whole community towards horrific deeds.

'Aham': I understand how societies can present good moral systems to adhere to but at times they can be prone to corruption. This takes me to my earlier question about clearly distinguishing between *Dharma* and *Adharma*. You used an example of an impersonator who pursues *Artha* even at the risk of harming others. However, I can think of other much trickier situations in life where I am not sure how to distinguish between *Dharma* and *Adharma*. For example, the war in *Mahābhārata* that ended up taking so many lives or the nuclear bombs dropped in Japan that killed so many but eventually became a key factor in the de-escalation of the second world war. How can one decide what is *Dharma* and what is *Adharma* in such cases?

In other situations, there could be multiple choices each of which may bring benefits to the world in different ways. For example, should a teacher aim to put his/her focus on teaching selected few bright students for maximising the efficiency and quality of knowledge sharing or should he/she aspire to reach out to the largest set of students possible? In that case, how should one decide? What's the correct path?

'Brahman': Let me make some general observations, and then I will comment on the specific example you have highlighted.

Firstly, control your senses and the ego-mind that create attachments and desires. Otherwise, they will interfere with the understanding of your *Personal Duties*. I will explain this further in a moment. Then be highly aware of your skills and capabilities and also of the professional/social environment and the situation around you. With those in mind, choose the way that allows you to walk the path of *Dharma,* i.e. supporting the harmonious functioning of the society/world in the best manner possible, as per your understanding. That becomes your *Swadharma*. Once you have recognised your *Swadharma* or your *Personal Duties*, work towards it with diligence and with absolute selflessness. As I had said before, everyone has to find his or her *Personal Duties* or *Swadharma*. You don't need to compare your *Swadharma* with that of others. Remember all duties stand on the same pedestal only differentiated by the spirit with which they are performed.

श्रेयान्स्वधर्मो विगुणः परधर्मात्स्वनुष्ठितात् ।
स्वभावनियतं कर्म कुर्वन्नाप्नोति किल्बिषम् ।।

Bhagavad Gita chapter 18 verse 47

It is better to act as per one's own dharma, even though imperfectly, than to do someone else's dharma, even though perfectly. By choosing to act as per Swadharma aligned to one's own nature, a person does not incur sin.

You took the example of the final battle of *Kurukshetra* in *Mahābhārata* and asked the question about *Dharma* and *Adharma*. In *Mahābhārata*, remember that war was not the first option and the point of the final war was reached only after all means to avoid the war had been exhausted. Once the two armies were facing each other in the battlefield, the *Personal Duty* of each and every warrior there was to fight the war itself! Think from their perspective. They possessed the skills and capabilities of a warrior. The war had to be ended and for the warriors, the only way to bring the war to an end was by defeating their enemy and that's what they did following their *Swadharma*. For the warriors on the side of *Pandavas*, their *Swadharma* was to defeat the *Kauravas* and for those on the side of *Kauravas*, their *Swadharma* was to defeat the *Pandavas*. People of both sides acted as per their *Swadharma*.

So, when you start to think from the perspective of *Swadharma*, you will know what you need to do. Also, your *Swadharma* will be very personal to you and maybe different from that of another person who is in the same environment. This is because even when in the same environment **everyone will have to choose their own path of *Swadharma* based on their own nature, skills, capabilities and experience**. People are not created equal and so they need not follow the same duties to contribute to the world.

Then you ask a question about a teacher - if it is better to be focused on a smaller group of students or should a teacher aim for educating a large group at the same time. With a large group of students, a teacher may not be able to give each student his/her personal attention but at least it would mean more students have access to the teacher at the same time. The two options require a different set of teaching styles, possibly different teaching platforms, suited for different types of subjects and also be driven by the specific student population. Based on all this information i.e. the environment and own teaching style/skills, the teacher needs to decide which according to him/her would be the best step forward. Both the paths lead to serving the students and thus are acts of *Dharma*. Stay true and stay committed to whichever path of *Dharma* that you choose. Once again, at the risk of repeating myself, I say that engage in acts of *Dharma*, work with selfless motives and don't spend time in indecision or inaction.

इति ते ज्ञानमाख्यातं गुह्याद्गुह्यतरं मया |
विमृश्यैतदशेषेण यथेच्छसि तथा कुरु ||

Bhagavad Gita chapter 18 verse 63
Commentary by Swami Mukundananda

Lord Krishna says, Thus, I have explained to you this knowledge that is more secret than all secrets. Ponder over it deeply, and <u>then do as you wish</u>.

Lord Ram made a similar statement to the residents of Ayodhya.

eka bāra raghunātha bolāe, guru dwija purabāsī saba āe (RaMāyān) [v34]

"Once, Lord Ram called all the residents of Ayodhya. Everyone, including Guru Vasishth came to hear him." In the discourse, Lord Ram explained to them the purpose of human life and the way to accomplish it. In the end, he concluded:

nahiṅ anīti nahiṅ kachhu prabhutāī, sunahu karahu jo tumhahi sohāī (RaMāyān) [v35]

"The advice I have given to you is neither incorrect nor coercive. Listen to it carefully, contemplate over it, and then <u>do what you wish</u>."

'Aham': I can see how important it is to keep a high level of awareness of one's own self and also the environment so that one always knows one's *Personal Duties*. At times though, our desires and attachments can distract us from our duties. Isn't it? Also, the definition of *Personal Duties* could change with time and circumstances. In that case, how do we know if there is a genuine need for change in *Personal Duties* or is it just attachments and ego-mind playing mischief?

'Brahman': Yes, it's a tricky situation to deal with. With time, people evolve, circumstances change and accordingly they affect one's duties as well. Beware that sometimes there is a need for genuine change in one's duties and other times, personal desires and attachments create a false picture of one's duties. One very popular example comes from the *Mahābhārata* when at the start of the war of

Kurukshetra, Arjuna[29] grew unwilling to carry out his duties because of his attachments with his family members and teachers, who stood as Arjuna's opponents in the war. His attachments and ignorance resulted in a delusion and he concluded that it's not his duty to participate in the war. Krishna came to his rescue. Krishna provided him with the knowledge and wisdom making him aware of his unnecessary attachments and delusions helping him realise his true *Personal Duties* or *Swadharma*. So, one always needs to be acutely aware of one's duties and be vigilant so that attachments and desires don't start interfering.

'Aham': Correctly deciphering one's *Swadharma* would indeed require a very high level of awareness. Since you have told me a lot of things about *Swadharma*, let me quickly recap to check if I have understood it correctly.

- Each person needs to decide one's *Swadharma* or *Personal Duties* for supporting the harmonious functioning of the world/society.

- With complete awareness of one's own nature, skills and capabilities, plus, with the accurate understanding of one's personal, social and professional environment one can discern the correct set of *Personal Duties*.

- *Swadharma* for a person doesn't remain constant but changes with time as there are changes in

---

[29] Arjuna and Krishna are characters from the epic Mahābhārata. Arjuna was considered the greatest archer. Krishna is an incarnation of Lord Vishnu.

one's environment and also in one's nature, skills and capabilities.

- Attachments and desires interfere with the correct understanding of one's *Swadharma*.

- One should act as per *Swadharma* with selfless motives and with a sense of duty. Of course, if actions are performed with selfish motives then those motives will bring commensurate consequences as per the *Law of Karma*.

- Avoid indecision and inaction.

'Brahman': Yes, that would be a fair summary.

'Aham': So, it seems that the answer to my question about my duty is to engage in carrying out acts of *Dharma*, and do so with selfless motives. Engaging in acts of *Dharma* needs to be my life's ultimate pursuit. Is that correct?

'Brahman': Yes, it is great to perform acts of *Dharma*. Though, even when undertaking the acts of *Dharma,* most remain engaged with their attachments of *Artha* and *Kāma*. That's not ideal for what we are trying to achieve. Let me share with you a practical tip to rise above selfish desires while performing acts of *Dharma*. Think about the higher ideal or the value your work will add towards harmonious, peaceful, efficient functioning of the world. I am sure in most situations you will be able to find a higher ideal for yourself which is beyond selfish benefits. Focus on that higher goal, the higher ideal. Think about how you can help to serve that higher goal. When that's purely what is driving your actions then you can walk the path of *Dharma* with selfless motives. In that situation, it is not the self-benefits that are driving your actions.

Now let me confess that this tip will help you to the path of *Dharma* alone but it will not completely liberate you from *Suffering* and bondages of your *Karma*. If you noticed I just said - "When that's purely what is driving your actions...", here it really means your actions are driven by your desire for goodness, your desire for being righteous. So the pursuit of *Dharma* is great but be aware of the catch that comes with it. Even acts of *Dharma* create binding effects if you have not freed yourself from the attachment to the acts of goodness. People who engage in the acts of *Dharma* often get attached to the goodness they are creating for society. They derive pleasure and pride from the contribution they are making to society. The ego becomes your primary enemy here. A doctor who is diligent and conscientious in his/her work starts to put him/herself on a God-like pedestal, a teacher par-excellence in every respect becomes proud of his/her knowledge and skills, and so on. Beware of the pride and pleasure being derived by your ego-mind in such cases. Attachments with any work or actions or their outcomes are all bondages.

If you want liberation from all *Sufferings* then you need to lose all attachments - no attachment even with the act of *Dharma* itself, nor even with the output of your work, i.e. the goodness you create, then that would lead you to the path of liberation from the *Karmic Cycle*, liberation from *Suffering*.

This is the eternal state of calm and bliss, free from any and all *Sufferings*[30]. We call this state as *Moksha*, the ultimate pursuit of human life. Undertaking acts of *Dharma* with selfless motives is an excellent tool to engage in *Nishkāma Karma*. Though, **don't get attached to the acts of *Dharma* itself and guide your actions with the knowledge of *Swadharma*. This, I tell you, is the path of *Karma Yoga* that leads to *Moksha* or path to *Liberation* from worldly *Sufferings*.**

Note that many learned men say that the successful pursuit of *Dharma* with no desires for *Kāma* or *Artha* is commendable. Only a few enlightened men/women get past it to attain *Moksha* or *Liberation* from the *Karmic Cycle* and *Suffering*.

'Aham': So, it's *Moksha* that is the ultimate pursuit. That is the eternal state of calm and bliss free of *Suffering* and *Misery*. Any and all attachments are essentially hurdles that stop us from attaining *Moksha*.

Also, you say that the path of *Dharma* gives us a tool to perform *Nishkāma Karma* but it's important not to get attached with the tool itself! As this will create another attachment. This is really important but when I think about it further, I feel that you are asking me to drop all that drives my *Karma*. You have gone beyond the objective of dropping all desires for self-benefits and now you are asking me to not even be attached with the higher ideal of creating

---

[30] You can refer back to the definition of *Sufferings* and *Miseries* in Chapter 2 - Attachments and Desires

goodness for the world. This is strange, and it is so for two reasons -

1. I am now back to square one because I don't know practically what will be the driver behind my actions... Surely not *Adharma*; not the desire for *Kāma*, not the desire for *Artha* as they create bondages, then what?

2. To attain *Moksha*, if I need to shed all desires, even the attachment with acts of *Dharma* then does it even matter what actions I am engaging in? If I don't even have the desire for *Dharma* then it doesn't matter what I do, it doesn't matter which path I take. I will randomly float around from one *Karma* to another. Isn't it so?

'Brahman': Well, that's a very good observation about shedding all desires, even shedding the attachment with *Dharma* and with the goodness created by such acts. *Moksha* is a state in which you are freed from all actions and also the consequences of all your actions. So what is the relevance of *Karma* in such a state? Let me share with you what drives one's *Karma* when in the state of *Moksha* or *Liberation*. How does it all work when there are no attachments/desires whatsoever driving your *Karma*...

Chapter 8 - Non-Resistance and Self-Sacrifice

'Brahman': You had asked me a few intriguing questions about what should ultimately drive one's *Karma*. We had discussed that even the acts of *Dharma* alone can't help attain *Liberation* or *Moksha*[31]. So what's the use of acting as per *Dharma*?

You have to act all the time - listen, think, talk, feel, walk, work and so on. While you can exist in this world without desires, you can't exist without *Karma*. Remember that all your attachments and desires are essentially products of your ego-mind working with your senses. When you lose all attachments, then in the absence of a driving desire, it is the knowledge of your *Personal Duties* or *Swadharma* that needs to guide your actions. Hence, the knowledge of your *Personal Duties* or *Swadharma* is so important and once you have understood that, it's all about working with a sense of duty. Working with equanimity, with no attraction or aversion but with pure diligence and conscientiousness. **It's the perfect knowledge of *Swadharma* that drives a *Karma Yogi* rather than attachments or desires of any sorts**.

In that state, there is no resistance. In that state, you have understood your *Swadharma* and you perform your duties with diligence. All this can happen only once you have worked through all your attachments

---

[31] This was discussed in the chapter on Duty

and desires - identified them and removed them. It's the final frontier. Once equipped with this knowledge and the experience of working diligently with a sense of duty, you need not resist anything that life throws at you as you approach them all with equanimity. Your response to all life situations through your *Karma* is equally spontaneous as you follow the clear and uncluttered path of *Swadharma*. Some call this experience of *Non-Resistance*[32] as 'flow' and some describe it as choiceless living.

...Such is the central idea of Karma-Yoga. The Karma-Yogi is the man who understands that the highest ideal is non-resistance....

...We all know that, if a certain number of us attempted to put that maxim fully into practice, the whole social fabric would fall to pieces, the wicked would take possession of our properties and our lives, and would do whatever they liked with us. Even if only one day of such non-resistance were practiced, it would lead to disaster...

...Before reaching this highest ideal, man's duty is to resist evil; let him work, let him fight, let him strike straight from the shoulder. Then only, when he has gained the power to resist, will non-resistance be a virtue...

- *Swami Vivekananda on Karma Yoga*

---

[32] Many times, the word Non-Resistance is used for Non-Violence. Here it is used as non-resistance to whatever needs doing and non-resistance to whatever comes your way in life.

'Aham': That means *Non-Resistance* is the highest ideal or highest virtue but it's not the first step but rather evidence that you have attained the ultimate pursuit of *Moksha*. Initially, one must overcome attachments and desires and learn to work in accordance with *Dharma*. Following the path of *Karma Yoga* equips one with the knowledge of his/her *Personal Duties* or *Swadharma* and also trains one to perform the duties diligently.

'Brahman': That's correct.

'Aham': You also describe *Non-Resistance* as a choiceless state? What does it mean?

'Brahman': Ordinarily, you always have three choices - to act, not to act and to act in
a different way[33]. On the path of *Karma Yoga,* you are purely guided by your *Swadharma* - your *Personal Duties*, with no other motive but for the sake of your duties alone. Once you have understood your *Swadharma*, there are no more choices to be made. That's why I say choiceless. Also, as you drop all attachments and desires then there are no preferred choices. All that comes in life is embraced with equanimity and dealt with as per *Swadharma*.

'Aham': How does one know if all the attachments and desires have been conquered and it's a reality rather than a delusion?

'Brahman': It's your unflinching awareness. You

---

[33] In Sanskrit it's called kartum shakyam, akartum shakyam and anyathaa kartum shakyam.

have to be astutely aware and honest about your motives and desires.

'Aham': Can you please help me summarise the characteristics of a *Karma Yogi* who has attained *Moksha*?

'Brahman': Sure. A *Karma Yogi* practices *Swadharma* with a sense of duty and in pursuit of excellence[34] and does so with complete non-attachment.

This complete non-attachment manifests in various ways -

- Without any attachments, there are no attractions or aversions so situations in life and all returns of work (*Karma-Phal*)[35] are equally welcome.

- With no attachments, there are no bondages. One is not bound by any desire and there is no resistance on the path of *Swadharma*.

- With no attachments, there are no selfish motives and hence there are no binding effects of *Karma* or consequences of *Karma* on one's own self, as the creator of consequences, that is desire, exists no more[36].

---

[34] Bhagavad Gita chapter 2 verse 50, noted in the chapter on Duty.

[35] Note, Returns of Work (*Karma-Phal*) is different from Result of Work as explained in the chapter on *Karma-Phal*.

[36] You can review the concept in the chapter on the *Law of*

- With no attachments, there are no desires to fulfil and hence a state of happiness or bliss is not conditional on the fulfilment of one's desires. Thus, an eternally blissful state is achieved as your natural blissful self exists uninhibited.

- Complete non-attachment also means no attachment with self. In such a state, *Swadharma* is practised for the benefit of others/world even at the cost of self. There is no fear either, as on the line of duty, one is committed to putting even one's own self at stake. You can pick any religion of the world and sacrificing oneself for other beings would be considered the highest ideal.

"...the very perfection of it is entire self-abnegation, readiness to sacrifice mind and body and everything for another being. When a man has reached that state, he has attained to the perfection of Karma-Yoga."
- *Swami Vivekananda on Non-Attachment and Self-Abnegation*

'Aham': So that's how *Karma Yoga* takes one to the final frontier of *Moksha* or the state of eternal bliss, free from *Suffering* where all attachments disappear including the attachment with one's own self! Losing the attachment with my mind and body sounds a bit tough though. Well, as you said, walking the path of *Dharma* with selfless motives is in itself commendable. Surely going a step beyond is only

---

Karma.

achieved by a rare few.

Well, overall, it does make sense to me but how would non-attachment manifest in one's life? Does a *Karma Yogi* renounce life itself, and not be interested in it? What does it mean in the real-world scenarios? Also, you mention about the unhindered existence of a naturally blissful self, what does that mean?

'Brahman': Non-attachment does not mean no *Karma*, but it means no attachment with *Karma*. It does not mean renouncing all experiences, but it means no attachment with them. Being free from attachments does not mean you have to stop being happy or stop engaging in activities of life. It only means you face life and all its experiences with equanimity. In the absence of attachments, you are not driven by them. No attachment means one is content with what life offers and accepts life without complaints or judgements.

Remember the life of lord Krishna who lived as a king with all the luxuries of life, he engaged in mischief as a child, fought wars, made friends, carried out his duties and dedicated his life to *Dharma*. He did all that but without incurring any binding effects of *Karma*.

You also ask about the naturally blissful self, yes, that's exactly how your 'true' self is. However, misguided by the senses and the ego-mind, you go searching for that happiness in the objects of sense-pleasure. Your senses and ego turn your pursuits outward into the material world-leading you to an unending chase that never gives you lasting happiness. We will talk about it further when we discuss *Māyā* and *Avidya*[37].

गतसङ्गस्य मुक्तस्य ज्ञानावस्थितचेतसः |
यज्ञायाचरतः कर्म समग्रं प्रविलीयते ||

Bhagavad gita Chapter 4 verse 23

Those who are unattached to material desires, have their intellect fixed in the divine knowledge, and perform all actions as a duty or sacrifice, they are freed from binding effects of Karma.

'Aham': I think I understand how non-attachment would manifest in the life of a *Karma Yogi*. Well, is this the only path to *Moksha*? And, why is there no reference to God? Is there no concept of God in Hinduism? If *Moksha* is considered the final frontier then where does God lead us to?

'Brahman': No this is not the only path but all paths lead to the same goal of *Moksha*. As you also brought up the topic of God, let me take this opportunity to talk about *Bhakti Yoga* - the path of Devotion and Love. This is another path that can take one to the same goal of *Moksha*.

Remember that these paths are not always exclusive of each other and rather very often overlap. Many times, people tread more than one path in their journey to *Moksha*. The ultimate goal, the state of Moksha, is exactly the same irrespective of the path

---

[37] Discussed in chapter 10 - Māyā and Avidya

71

taken.

"The Karma-Yogi need not believe in any doctrine whatever. He may not believe even in God, may not ask what his soul is, nor think of any metaphysical speculation. He has got his own special aim of realising selflessness; and he has to work it out himself. Every moment of his life must be realisation, because he has to solve by mere work, without the help of doctrine or theory, the very same problem to which the Gyani[38] applies his reason and inspiration and the Bhakta[39] his love."

- *Swami Vivekananda on Not-Attachment and Self-Abnegation*

---

[38] Follower of *Gyan Yoga*. This has been discussed further in chapter 12.

[39] Follower of *Bhakti Yoga*. This has been discussed further in chapter 9.

Chapter 9 - Path of Love

When all thoughts, all words, and all deeds are given up unto the Lord, and the least forgetfulness of God makes one intensely miserable, then love has begun. This is the highest form of love because therein is no desire for reciprocity, which desire is in all human love.

- *Swami Vivekananda on Bhakti Yoga*

'Brahman': You asked me about God and the role of God in life and in attainment of *Moksha*. This is a very popular path, I must say. Many wise men have said that *Bhakti Yoga* is the most natural path for all humans as it doesn't restraint in any way. In fact, it just gives a higher, more powerful direction to all human attachments and desires. The idea is simple, a sense of desire and longing is always there in all humans, though it is usually directed towards a sense-object. In *Bhakti Yoga*, this desire and longing is re-directed towards God, away from the desires of senses and ego. This is the path of worship, devotion, love.

This path of Love, also called *Bhakti Yoga*, essentially teaches complete surrender while practicing the most intense love. I will explain to you how **the ultimate pursuit of God on the path of *Bhakti Yoga* leads one into the realms of deep, profound, unconditional love.** We have already discussed how *Moksha* or *Liberation* from *Suffering and Misery* is the ultimate objective of human life so let's now focus on how *Bhakti Yoga* leads one to the path of *Moksha*.

'Aham': I am curious to know more but I am also concerned if this is a path of blind faith which is against all scientific and analytical temperament. This path could be easily exploited if your ideals are not right or are incorrectly interpreted.

'Brahman': The idea of worshipping a God or being completely devoted to one, has a natural appeal to large masses as it provides a relatable and concrete object to focus on, to love, to admire, to dedicate oneself to. To an ordinary man, it's much more difficult to go out in search of abstract ideas or knowledge and truth (*Gyan Yoga*[40]). Similarly renouncing all worldly attachments and desires are equally difficult to attain (*Karma Yoga*). *Bhakti Yoga*, gives you a way to channel your desires in the direction of a higher ideal - i.e. your God in this case.

The one great advantage of Bhakti is that it is the easiest and the most natural way to reach the great divine end in view; its great disadvantage is that in its lower forms it oftentimes degenerates into hideous fanaticism.

- *Swami Vivekananda on Bhakti Yoga*

However, as you said, sometimes *Bhakti* may lead to fanatical behaviour where one can only accept his or her own ideal and reject all others. To a practitioner

---

[40] Also written as *Jñāna Yoga*. We will learn about it further in the subsequent chapters.

of *Bhakti Yoga*, this feeling of disrespect or even hatred for others must act as a reminder that his/her own love or devotion has still not culminated. When the highest form of love is reached all hatred disappears. This may sound like a gospel for now but I will provide you more insights as we go along.

That singleness of attachment (Nishthā) to a loved object, without which no genuine love can grow, is very often also the cause of the denunciation of everything else. All the weak and undeveloped minds in every religion or country have only one way of loving their own ideal, i.e. by hating every other ideal...

...At one time, in India, representatives of different sects met together and began to dispute. One said that the only God was Shiva; another said, the only God was Vishnu, and so on; and there was no end to their discussion. A sage was passing that way, and was invited by the disputants to decide the matter. He first asked the man who was claiming Shiva as the greatest God, "Have you seen Shiva? Are you acquainted with Him? If not, how do you know He is the greatest God?" Then turning to the worshipper of Vishnu, he asked, "Have you seen Vishnu?" And after asking this question to all of them, he found out that not one of them knew anything of God. That was why they were disputing so much, for had they really known, they would not have argued....

- *Swami Vivekananda on Bhakti Yoga*

The other important aspect is to choose a worthy ideal. Otherwise, your *bhakti* or love could never be channeled in the right direction. So how does one select a worthy ideal? Everyone has their own intrinsic nature that drives the selection of one or more ideals to dedicate oneself to. Such chosen God(s) are also called *Personal God(s)* or *Ishta Devta*. Worshipping some form of God to fulfil selfish desires typically forms the humble beginning of *Bhakti Yoga*. This should certainly not be the end though on the path of *Bhakti*.

कामैस्तैस्तैर्हृतज्ञानाः प्रपद्यन्तेऽन्यदेवताः |
तं तं नियममास्थाय प्रकृत्या नियताः स्वया ||

Bhagavad Gita chapter 7 verse 20

Those whose wisdom has been distorted by material desires surrender to the demi/celestial gods. They practice particular rules and rituals that are driven by their own nature.

'Aham': You say that driven by one's desires, a devotee initially chooses his/her *Personal God(s)*. This presumably is because of faith in the *Personal God(s)* that the devotee's desires will be fulfilled. This sounds very relatable. Then you say that this only forms the humble beginnings of *Bhakti Yoga*. Then what comes next?

'Brahman': Interestingly, *Bhakti Yoga* has a unique peculiarity - properly undertaking this path and persevering with it automatically results in spiritual evolution. I will explain this to you.

While everyone can claim to love and worship a God,

it's important for the devotee to understand what the path of *Bhakti Yoga* truly entails. It is easy to talk about love and much more difficult to 'be' in love. The path of *Bhakti* usually begins with a duality of devotee and God. At this stage it's purely <u>faith</u> that the devotee has in God, and often it's the faith that his/her desires will be fulfilled by a powerful God such as the desire for wealth, health, success, luck, happiness, etc. This is often a form of God of the devotees' choosing, called *Personal God* or *Ishta Devta*[41]. *Ishta Devta* represents the provider of reward or return that is being sought. This is considered the lower form of *Bhakti*, also called *Apara Bhakti*. In such a state the idea of devotion is narrow and conditional. This faith is also rooted in desires and ego.

In early stages of *Bhakti*, having complete devotion for an abstract idea of God is extremely difficult. So one takes the help of symbols, rituals, prayers, idols, books, bells, music, images, temples, and so on. Anything that can be easily perceived by the senses, anything that helps to form a concrete image of the abstract, is used for worship. Societies around the world use different symbols that personifies the values that the devotee is seeking. There is nothing

---

[41] The word *Ishta* is derived from the root Ish, to desire, choose. *Ishta Devta* is a god of one's own choosing that's why it's also called *Personal God*. In Hinduism, many forms of Gods have been referenced that are often called deities, celestial gods, etc. and each of them typically represent certain values, personality and power. This helps devotees to initially engage with and focus on a form of God which naturally aligns with their thoughts and desires. For example, Goddess Laxmi is often worshipped by those who desire wealth and prosperity.

wrong in the use of symbols as it helps the untrained mind to focus on an object that represents the values that the devotee seeks. It does go wrong however, when that's where the devotion ends!

'Aham': That's interesting as in the early stages, God is very much worshipped for the fulfilment of worldly desires. I can see so many such cases around me. I think that for most, the journey of worship and devotion ends right there.

'Brahman': Yes, you are correct. For most devotees, worship remains limited to an ask for fulfillment of desires and fear of losing what one already has or desires to have. In the early stages **when worldly desires are still the key driver in one's life, praying to any God will not relieve one of the** *Sufferings*. The solution offered by *Bhakti Yoga* is to work and live with a spirit of dedicating all the desires to the *Personal God*. Harboring this feeling of dedicating all actions and returns of actions to God helps in gradually getting over those desires. **When material desires are considered not for personal enjoyment but as an offering to God, the attachment with those material desires start to weaken.** This is something that you can very easily put to practice and test for yourself.

In this way, the journey of a *Bhakta*[42] continues.

'Aham': Why does the journey continue though? What is that force that keeps the devotee going even when the desires for material gains start to weaken?

---

[42] Follower of *Bhakti Yoga*.

'Brahman': It's the longing and love for God. It's the natural course that love takes for anyone. If there is intense longing and love for someone, this is the natural way in which love evolves. Gradually love for God starts to become an objective in itself. In fact, as the love grows stronger, the devotee realises that any and all attachments and desires of ego-mind and senses become an impediment to pure bonding with God. Clearly, the single-minded longing for God can only take place when your mind and heart are free from all distractions. All attachments and desires of senses and ego-mind create distractions. In that state, a *bhakta* is not bothered about any material desires or sense-pleasures.

Think of it yourself and you may be able to find examples of such intense love from your own life. In such situations the lover can think of nothing else but the beloved. Nothing else matters. It even reaches a state when there is no care for self and the lover is completely overwhelmed with the thoughts of the beloved. That level of intense love can't coexist with one's attachments and desires for anything else in life, be it wealth, name, fame, power, authority, lust, greed, pride, or any other desire. All such desires are distractions which have no place any more as all that remains is the most intense longing for the beloved.

As the love for God grows stronger, the cause of *Suffering* - attachments and desires - fall away. The love for God keeps getting stronger and it does so for no material rewards but purely for the love of God.

Along with material desires, the other thing that

drops with it is fear. Love can't be forced through fear. God is no longer seen as someone with a carrot (desired rewards) in one hand and stick (punishment) in the other. This means the devotee is now neither driven by desires nor by fear. When both worldly desires and fear are gone, pure love for God blossoms.

'Aham': This is truly a transformational journey that you are talking about. Let me summarise this. You say that the devotion that begins with faith in a God of one's own choosing, i.e. a *Personal God* or *Ishta Devta*, gets transformed over the course of *Bhakti Yoga*. Initially, a devotee chooses a *Personal God* that personifies the values close to his/her own nature and resonates with the devotee's own worldly desires. That is perhaps why I hear about so many worshipping and praying for the fulfilment of their desires. Also, who they worship changes with what is desired!

But then in the due course, you say that, as the devotee persists on the path of *Bhakti*, the devotion and longing for God grows stronger, and all worldly desires fall away. The bond with God is no longer for personal benefits or even out of fear. That is a state with no desire or fear, thus, the devotee would graciously welcome whatever comes his/her way in life as he/she is not bothered about anything other than the longing for God. At this point, love for God remains, even though the very reasons behind the initial connection with God has become irrelevant for the devotee as he/she loses all worldly desires.

That's really interesting as the bond between the devotee and his/her *Personal God* grows stronger even though the very reason why the devotee chose that *Personal God* doesn't exist anymore!

'Brahman': That's true. That's the transformational power of love that takes over the devotee. In fact, love alters the equation between the devotee and his/her *Personal God* and even changes the perception of God itself. This happens as the love intensifies further. Love itself becomes the highest ideal being pursued. When you love someone so greatly, you are blinded by it. When you are completely in love with someone, you can't judge them anymore, you can't judge their qualities, it doesn't matter what they offer you and what they demand from you. The same happens with the devotees's *Personal God*. There is a 'new' realisation of God or a new avatar of God that is no longer identified by the qualities that the devotee's *Personal God* or *Ishta Devta* initially represented. In spite of that, there still exists the most intense love for the beloved. This new avatar is often given different names such as - Supreme God, Impersonal God, Formless God, *Brahman*, etc.

The realisation of this new avatar has been described in various ways but if you look from the perspective of a *bhakta*, it is just pure and all-pervasive love that remains in the devotee-God relationship. This is an intense, all-absorbing love where the devotee surrenders his/her own self. It's actually a natural outcome of the highest form of love that can be pursued by any person. For those on the path of *bhakti*, there is nothing else in life of any relevance but the longing for the *Brahman* - which pervades everything in the world with its limitless presence.

'Aham': What do you mean when you say that *Brahman* or the *Supreme God* feels all pervasive to a *Bhakta*?

'Brahman': It's just the very nature of love. Think of a mother whose child has left the city for work or education. In the absence of her child, so often her heart would get filled with utmost love and memories of her beloved when she sees the child's toys or clothes or the child's room. It feels to her that she can see her child in all these objects that she associates with her child. Similarly, for a true *bhakta*, out of pure and boundless love for God, it's not surprising that anything and everything in the world evokes the love and memories of God. A bhakta is able to see God in every particle of the universe and it is driven purely by the power of love.

एवं सर्वेषु भूतेषु भक्तिरव्यभिचारिणी।
कर्तव्या पण्डितैर्ज्ञात्वा सर्वभूतमयं हरिम्॥

Knowing that Hari, the Lord, is in every being, the wise have thus to manifest unswerving love towards all beings.
- *Vishnupuran*

'Aham': Is that the highest level of love for God?

'Brahman': No there is another step but this is the rarest of rare phenomena with no other equivalence or analogy that I can draw to explain it to you. You will have to walk this path yourself to realise it or else my words will only sound like gospel.

In the highest state of love, not just the outside world but eventually even the self feels part of the Supreme God or *Brahman*. The love of a *bhakta* culminates in the feeling of one-ness with God as there is nothing including one's own self that is felt separate from God. The love and the belongingness to the beloved is so intense that duality between the devotee and the God disappears. This is called Tadiyatā (Oneness) the highest level of *Bhakti* or *Para Bhakti*. It is free from any kind of motive and is purely for the sake of love alone. There are no desires, simply unconditional love. Love becomes all-pervasive as the whole world looks immersed in love and seems part of the beloved including one's own self.

Shri Ramakrishna Paramhansa said -
"You must accept all these – God with form and God without form. I was meditating in the Kali Temple when I saw Ramani, a prostitute. I said to the Divine Mother, 'Mother, you have this form too!' That is why I say you must accept all. You can never tell when She may appear before you in any form She likes."

In this all-pervasive love, any and all differences between all beings disappear as they seem to be part of God, including devotee's own self. There is no need for temples or mantras or any other rituals or symbols as one can then experience God everywhere. This intense all-absorbing love brings the feeling of perfect self-surrender. There are no preferences or choices to be made. Everything is accepted with equanimity. Pain and pleasure are both equally welcome. There are no desires left, no fear left either and the ego-self gets completely dissolved in the Supreme God or *Brahman*.

That love of God grows and assumes a form which is

called Para-Bhakti or supreme devotion. Forms vanish, rituals fly away, books are superseded; images, temples, churches, religions and sects, countries and nationalities — all these little limitations and bondages fall off by their own nature from him who knows this love of God.
- *Swami Vivekananda on Bhakti Yoga*

'Aham': Lastly, shall I say, through *Bhakti Yoga*, you reach the same state of *Moksha* as you do with *Karma Yoga*?

'Brahman': You do indeed. As you would have noticed in the journey of *Bhakti Yoga* that I described to you, you may start off with worshipping your *Personal God* for the fulfilment of your desires and attachments but all desires drop along the way. There is no ego left as the sense of self merges with the Supreme *(Tadiyatā[43])*, there are no worldly attachments left. Just an intense, unconditional love for God remains. With the ego and attachments gone, you can see the true reality, the Supreme God, the *Brahman*. All you are concerned about is the love for God. You feel the oneness with God[44]. There is no resistance or attraction anymore for anything that life throws at you. Everything is accepted with equanimity as the will of God. In that stage with no worldly attachments and complete self-surrender, you simply feel that you and everything around you in this world are nothing more but a conduit to

---

[43] Oneness

[44] This is part of the Advaita (Non-Dual) philosophy. As per the Dvaita (Duality) philosophy, the devotee never has this feeling of oneness and forever remains separate from God.

express the will of God. With such surrender and love there can be nothing that can bother you.

Rahim Khankhana was a famous poet saint, during the Mughal period in Indian history. Some say that he was a great devotee of Lord Krishna. It is immaterial in this context, but what is important though is his devotion to God. Peculiarly, when he would give alms in charity, he would lower his eyes. It is said that Saint Tulsidas heard of Rahim's style of giving alms, and asked him:

aisī denī dena jyuñ, kita sīkhe ho saina
jyoṅ jyoṅ kara ūñchyo karo, tyoṅ tyoṅ niche naina

"Sir, where did you learn to give alms like this? Your hands are as high as your eyes are low." Rahim replied beautifully and in all humbleness:

denahāra koī aur hai, bhejata hai dina raina
loga bharama hama para kareṅ, yāte niche naina

"The giver is someone else, giving day and night. But the world gives me the credit, and so I lower my eyes."

Thus, you can see the commonalities even though this time you approach *Moksha* through the path of most intense and unconditional love for God.

- There are no attachments and desires of the senses and the ego-mind left in you.

- There is no affinity or aversion to anything that life throws at you. Every situation is accepted with equanimity.

- The Ego-Self is lost as it is dissolved in the all-consuming love. As you lose your own self in love, there are no more fears, no more wants.

- All you are left with is the bliss of an undying, unconditional love.

'Aham': I can see how the path of love takes one to the same state of *Moksha*, that is reached through *Karma Yoga* by the selfless practice of *Swadharma*. Though, in practical life scenarios do we not have someone following both the paths at the same time?

'Brahman': Oh yes it does happen. Almost everyone starts from a place where one is full of worldly attachments and desires. Even when one knows that these attachments create all sorts of *Sufferings*, they are still extremely difficult to renounce. It ain't easy to develop the highest sense of awareness that can help one to recognise and then renounce all attachments and desires. So, working in a way that all the desired returns are dedicated to God can help in the initial stages of *Karma Yoga*. Similarly, for those who are more inclined towards *Bhakti Yoga*, but are still bound to carry out his/her personal, social and professional duties, the awareness of *Swadharma* helps them to stay on the righteous path and learn to work with the right spirit and a sense of duty. Eventually all paths merge into one state of non-attachment and selflessness that we call *Moksha*.

'Aham': You have now explained to me two ways of reaching the state of *Moksha* - one is through performing your *Personal Duties* and the other is through worship or *Bhakti*. You also mentioned a path of *Gyan Yoga*. Could you please tell me more about it?

'Brahman': *Gyan Yoga* is the pursuit of knowledge. It's the path of self-knowledge and self-realisation. Once again, it leads to the same ultimate goal of *Moksha* or *Liberation*. But what is there to know that you do not know already? Let's try to explore this further...

Chapter 10 - Māyā and Avidya

'Brahman': Before we begin exploring the path of *Gyan Yoga*, I must warn you that this may take you to unfamiliar albeit still very practical and tangible territory. This involves a lot of thinking, contemplation and analysis of things in life that you have always taken for granted. This is about questioning even the most familiar things in life that you have learnt to live with. Hence, do expect to go out of your comfort zone and genuinely ask some truly profound questions about your own being.

'Aham': Sure. I am ready. Please tell me more.

'Brahman': As I said, *Gyan Yoga* is about asking some profound questions about your own being. But then why ask such questions at all? What's the need? To understand this, we need to take a step back. Take a very conscious look at the world that you are living in. When you get too used to an environment, you stop questioning it. When you get too close to your environment, you sometimes start to lose the perspective. I want you to ask questions about your environment, the world that you live in and re-build your understanding of the world around you.

'Aham': Ok sure. Though I will need your guidance.

'Brahman': Let me help your thinking by showing the world around you in a new light. Earlier, we discussed the ideas and experiences of the most intense and intoxicating love there can be. Needless to say, it can't be understood until experienced. This time I am starting from something that you must have experienced already - *Māyā*.

So often you would have heard people using the word *Māyā* to describe the world or the universe. *Māyā* is often translated into words such as illusion, deception, trick or magic. But what does it truly mean when one says that the world is an illusion or magic?

Let's first try to understand the subtle meaning of the word *Māyā* and then we will discuss why it's such an important philosophical concept to understand.

When the world or the universe is said to be *Māyā* or illusion it doesn't mean that the universe or the world doesn't exist or is unreal or it is just a figment of one's imagination and nothing else. *Māyā* simply signifies the 'appearance' of the world or the way the world appears to work. It's a comment about the way the world is perceived.

'Aham': If *Māyā* is simply a factual representation of the way the world is perceived then why this connotation of illusion?

'Brahman': Let me explain to you with some practical examples. Historically, *Māyā* has been defined in many different ways but mostly in metaphysical terms. Let me take a different approach and give you a few examples[45] that shows how *Māyā* works in the

---

[45] Examples adapted from Swami Vivekananda's lectures on *Māyā*.

real world. Then decide its meaning for yourself. Here you go -

Death is the ultimate reality. Everyone who is alive today has to die. This is an unchangeable reality that every adult is fully aware of. Still, you will find that people have a tremendous clinging or attachment to life. It is not as innocuous as it might appear to be. This is in fact one of the most profound factors that fundamentally distorts people's perspective of life. Fear, anxiety, stress, greed, selfishness, wants and what not does it add to one's life... If you think about it, you will wonder why such attachment to something that is transient, temporary? Is there an unexplainable illusion driving everyone? This is *Māyā*.

People across class, community, country, sex and race are always chasing happiness through their material desires and sense-pleasures. Even when the desire is fulfilled the promised happiness never comes or if it comes it doesn't last. And then another chase for another desire begins. It's a futile chase that never ends in lasting happiness or satisfaction. Still the chase goes on. Why? What can explain this? This is *Māyā*.

A mother is always fond of her child, and even if her child grows up to become an absolute brute, she still fails to lose her attachment. Even when she notices her child's ill-doings and she wants to break away, she absolutely can't. She covers up saying it's love, but this is bondage. The fact is even if she wants, she can't break that bondage. This is *Māyā*.

You feel that you are acting by free will. Is there really a free will or is it the will of your attachments created by the senses and ego-mind[46] that drives you, while you think it's your free-will. So how free is your 'free will'? People live their whole life never realising the limits of their free will. This is *Māyā*.

People see this world in terms of good and bad, whatever your understanding of good and bad may be. More importantly, isn't good and bad only relative to each other? Doesn't good and bad depend on who is judging it? For a child who got burnt - fire is bad, for a cook - fire is good. So is fire good or bad? Goat eats grass, tiger eats goat. Who is good and who is bad? If judgement changes with the judge, with time, with place, then why this constant urge to judge - good and bad? What will be achieved? This is *Māyā*.

Man has always found new pleasures of senses and ego. As the level of pleasure increases so does the pain of losing it. It soon becomes a zero-sum game. But the same process continues forever defeating all rationality. This is *Māyā*.

The world is full of these contradictions and many more. *Māyā* simply states those facts as they exist. The facts are so obvious but still for almost everyone, life is a continuous struggle through one or more of such paradoxical traps. What keeps the world going like this forever? If you can see and understand the traps, you will wonder why people behave so

---

[46] The influence or control of attachments and desires on one's *Karma* was discussed in *chapter 2 - Attachments and Desires* and *chapter 3 - Karma-Phal*

irrationally. Some say it's an illusion because it feels like a mirage that people keep chasing. However, *Māyā* is better described as the way this world 'appears' to function.

Māyā is a statement of the fact of this universe, of how it is going on.
  - *Swami Vivekananda on Māyā*

'Aham': I can certainly see the contradictions or the paradoxes. But what can explain this behaviour prevalent in almost every person and it has gone on like this forever? How to deal with it? Of course, one can say that - yes, these traps are hard facts, you don't know why they are there but don't bother. All one needs to do is carry on experiencing whatever little pleasure one can get in life. Yes, it comes with suffering but so what. Life has always gone on like this and will continue in future as well. Isn't this the practical wisdom? The good thing is that it gives you hope, false it may be, but there is hope. Hope that there will be happiness. Hope that good things will happen to you eventually.

'Brahman': Well, what you have explained as practical wisdom is exactly the path taken by almost everyone when they face the question of dealing with *Māyā* in their lives. Yes, people do try to live this life with a false hope. As a young kid hopes are high, but it diminishes as you age. However, people keep sticking to it.

There is another option though, and that is to

confront it. Accept the traps but resolve to escape because you can't live with a lie, a false hope, all your life. When the longing for truth is so intense that it feels better to die in search of truth than to not try at all, then comes the hope of realising the ultimate truth, the possibility of escaping the trap of *Māyā*.

When Buddha sat under the bodhi tree, with the idea of practicality, he rejected it as non-sense, even though he did not have a way out. He was tempted to give up his quest and go back to his old life. But the old life signified fraud, a life of lies spoken daily to one's own self. He said "Death is better than a vegetating ignorant life; it is better to die on the battle-field than to live a life of defeat." This is the basis of religion.[47]

Remember that *Māyā* doesn't provide an explanation or a solution but it just states what exists. Though, recognising and acknowledging *Māyā* or the contradictory/paradoxical traps of life is the first step towards escaping these traps.

'**Aham**': Then please tell me how to escape these traps. And why is it so difficult to escape the trap of *Māyā*?

'**Brahman**': I have just explained to you how *Māyā* manifests itself in this world in the most paradoxical of ways. Ultimately, it's you who is constantly living in this trap, looking for happiness in this trap. There must be something in you that makes you go on like this.

---

[47] Adapted from Swami Vivekananda's lectures on *Maya* and *Gyan Yoga*

'Aham': Yes, that sounds like a logical argument. It's intriguing why I can't escape *Māyā* even when I know the traps it is weaving.

'Brahman': As we have seen, *Māyā* affects everything in this world. It is all pervading and has existed forever. To understand how all the beings remain trapped in the world of *Māyā*, you need to understand two other concepts - *Avidya* or *Ignorance* and *Guna* or *Innate Qualities*. Let me explain both of these to you.

I will begin by asking you a simple question. If I ask you to identify or define yourself, how would you do that?

'Aham': Depends on what you want to know. I have many identities. My name identifies me. My surname signifies the family and even the community I belong to. My family and relationships also add to my identity. My language and the region I come from shape my identity. I am proud of them all. My profession, my accomplishments, my job-title and my values are also my identity. My knowledge, skills, aspirations and desires make me who I am. Of course, I am also the body I look at in the mirror. They are all apt to be called my identity and together they describe me as a person who is me, distinct from everyone else. They describe me as a unique being.

'Brahman': This is what I expected. It's common to identify with all those attributes. Whether the way you identify yourself is right or wrong is a secondary question. The primary question is - what is it that you are trying to identify? Think about it long and hard.

When you identify yourself with your body, your thoughts, your beliefs, your country, your profession, your religion and so on, I see them as different layers of paint put on a canvass. You can paint the canvas whichever way you like. You can change the colours, you can even remove some and add others. Though, what I am interested in is not the paint but the canvas itself. What lies beneath the layers of paint? What is it at the deepest level of your own - 'self'? That is what I am after.

You will notice that the way you identify yourself could change over time. Then what's it that has stayed constant and will remain so with time? Is there any such thing?

Swami Sivananda Saraswati Maharaj explains the Brahma-Sutra stating that -
"You identify yourself with the body and say, 'I am fair, dark, stout or thin. I am a Brahmin, I am a Kshatriya, I am a doctor'.
You identify yourself with the senses and say, 'I am blind, I am dumb'.
You identify yourself with the mind and say, 'I know nothing. I know everything. I became angry. I enjoyed a good meal. I am suffering from this disease'.

The entire object of the Brahma Sutras is to remove this erroneous identification of the Soul with the body which is the root cause of your sufferings and miseries, which is the product of Avidya (ignorance) and help you in the attainment of the final emancipation through knowledge of Brahman."

'Aham': I understand your question but I don't think

I have an answer. I don't know of any other identity deeper than those that I have just described.

'Brahman': That's ok. That's the beginning - to know that there is something that you don't know! The way you identify yourself has been built by your ego-mind with the help of inputs from your environment[48]. This is called *Avidya* or *Ignorance*. Pursuit of self-knowledge will help you overcome this *Ignorance*.

As soon as you start identifying with your body, your mind, your thoughts/feelings and your possessions, the very next step is to feel a need to preserve them, protect them, save them; and that immediately brings selfishness. What you seem to be identifying with are finite, destructible, damageable and hence those urges to save and protect are natural. This is how *Avidya* manifests itself in your life. We have already discussed how selfishness or selfish desires lead to *Suffering[49]*. It pushes you away from the highest ideal of self-sacrifice and self-abnegation[50].

The other important concept that you need to learn in order to understand how this world works and why it does so is - *Guna* or *Innate Qualities*. Everyone in this world is characterised by his/her *Innate Qualities*.

Do you remember our discussion about attachments

---

[48] Taking inputs through one or more of the 5 senses.

[49] Discussed in the chapter on Attachments and Desires.

[50] This was discussed in the chapter on Non-Resistance and Self-Sacrifice.

and desires?

'Aham': Yes, I do.

'Brahman': When we discuss *Guna* you will see what drives specific attachments and desires and thus people's *Karma*[51]. Normally, for almost everyone, *Avidya* and *Guna* characterise the 'self'. *Gyan*[52] *Yoga* is the path of knowledge that helps you understand your 'true' self, your 'true' nature and it helps you break-free from *Avidya* and *Guna*.

'Aham': Please tell me about *Guna* and the path of *Gyan Yoga*.

There is a terrible degeneration of consciousness in the case of the individual earthly being.
It first forgets the Reality; secondly it centres its consciousness in a localised body; thirdly it drags other external bodies also to its own self and regards such of the few as are beneficial to its egoistic pleasures as its own self and consequently begins to hate those entities or individuals which are not connected with its interests or which are set in opposition to it.
  -   Moksha Gita by Swami Sivananda

---

[51] Until they have achieved *Moksha*.

[52] Gyan (/gjɑːn/; ज्ञान) literally means knowledge.

Chapter 11 - Guna (Innate Qualities)

'Brahman': We were discussing *Māyā, Avidya* and *Guna*. Various explanations have been given to describe the relationship between the three. We saw how *Māyā* becomes visible through many paradoxical traps that exist in this world. We have discussed how you associate with the identities created by your ego-mind and your inability to see your 'true' self. We described this as *Avidya*. Furthermore, it's the *Guna* within you that makes you act in ways that keep you trapped in *Māyā*.

Guna means '*Innate Qualities*' or '*Natural Tendencies*'. Each and every one carries three kinds of *Guna* - *Tamas, Rajas, Sattva*. All the three *Guna* are always present in everyone but vary in their relative amounts or influence. The work of all *Guna* is to create bondages i.e. all of them create attachments that you naturally cling on to. Together they drive the nature or personality and outlook of a person. **Māyā manifests in this world through the presence of *Guna* or *Innate Qualities* in every being.** You will see that due to the effects of *Guna* you remain entangled in the paradoxical traps of *Māyā*.

Let's first have a look at the three *Guna* and then we will explore their effects on human life. After that, we will look into ways to escape the effects of *Guna* and break the traps of *Māyā*.

Tamas represents inactivity, apathy, indifference, shame, pity, malice, fear and ignorance. *Tamasic* qualities can force one to be inactive, depressed and lazy. It can cause mala fide thoughts and intentions. It leads to acts of ignorance where one acts without understanding the consequences of one's actions.

Rajas represents passion, anger and energy. *Rajas* guna causes the mind to be restless and forces activity or work that kills idleness. *Rajas* guna wants new levels and types of enjoyment, sensation, and variety. One can rarely find peace with this state of mind. *Rajas* is responsible for anxiety, stress, arrogance, lust, jealousy, greed and so on.

Sattva manifests itself as peace, calmness, balance, knowledge and harmony. It is the quality of goodness and contentment. It is free of fear, greed, anger and malice. It is pure and forgiving. With *Sattva* guna one is not dependent on sensual pleasures and material desires to feel happy, content or peaceful.

It's the presence and mix of these *Guna* that drive your natural tendencies to act in certain ways or hold certain attachments and desires.

'Aham': You say that ultimately all *Guna* create attachments of different kinds driving one's *karma*. So it must also determine one's likes and dislikes. Correct?

'Brahman': Yes, *Guna* is intrinsically linked to your likes and dislikes, your attachments and desires. Though I must add here that **one can definitely and consciously alter the mix of *Guna* in oneself.** Contemplating and meditating on your *Guna* will help you reveal why you have certain likes and dislikes, certain attachments and desires. Conversely, consciously altering your likes and dislikes and attachments and desires have an effect on your *Guna*.

The degree to which each of the three *Guna* are present or active in a person at a given point in time drives his/her thoughts, intentions and actions. So it's extremely important to be alert and be conscious of the impact of *Guna* on yourself. It's the interplay of the three *Guna in you* that drives all your *Karma* i.e. your thoughts, feelings and actions.

'Aham': Ok, that sounds logical to me. I think I have also started to see the link between *Guna* driving one's personality traits and even one's pursuits of life[53].

'Brahman': Yes, that's correct.

When *Rajas* dominates, then expect the person to be driven with passion and energy chasing one's desires. In such cases, people are in pursuit of *Artha* and *Kāma*. Their life will be full of energy, passion, desire, stress, anxiety, sorrow, anger, excitement, envy, jealousy and so on. They are likely to be greedy and in a hurry to act in order to fulfil their desires. Their attachments would often shroud their intellect and judgement, making them act in self-interest.

If a person is driven by *Sattvic* qualities, then expect him/her to engage in acts of *Dharma* without any

---

[53] Refer to the chapter on Duty to learn more about the pursuits of human life (*Puruṣārtha*).

selfish desires. Such people embody spiritual knowledge and goodness. They show high awareness of their actions and fully comprehend the consequences of their actions. They have a strong sense of duty and responsibility. They approach all *Karma* with equanimity and remain undisturbed in success and failure. They learn, they improve, and act with no remorse. They work for the sake of work and for the sake of higher ideals rather than self-interest. They are not driven by fear or greed.

People with dominant *Tamasic* qualities can tend to avoid *Swadharma* and even step outside the realms of *Dharma* i.e. he or she may create discord and disharmony. Inactivity, apathy, indifference, negativity, depression are all tamasic qualities. Due to such qualities, their work is often characterised by inefficiency, insincerity, and imperfection. Such people often engage in simple repetitive jobs and resist change. They focus on their fears and pains and use them to justify their behaviour.

As I said before, all three *Guna* are always present in everyone in different proportions but can be altered consciously. Usually, a mix of *Guna* are active at a time and their combination drives the *Karma*. It's worth noting that, if one has elements of *Tamas Guna*, it doesn't mean all the *Tamasic* characteristics will be present but yes some of the characteristics will definitely be there and if, say, *Tamas* is the dominant *Guna* in any person then some of those *Tamasic* qualities will be truly intense and a major driving force in the person's life. The same goes with the presence of the other *Guna* as well.

नियतं सङ्गरहितमरागद्वेषतः कृतम् ।
अफलप्रेप्सुना कर्म यत्तत्सात्त्विकमुच्यते ॥

यत्तु कामेप्सुना कर्म साहंकारेण वा पुनः ।
क्रियते बहुलायासं तद्राजसमुदाहृतम् ॥

अनुबन्धं क्षयं हिंसामनपेक्ष्य च पौरुषम् ।
मोहादारभ्यते कर्म यत्तत्तामसमुच्यते ॥

Bhagavad Gita, Chapter 18, verses 23–25

Action that is in accordance with duty, which is performed without attachment, without love or hate, by one who has renounced fruitive results, is called action in the mode of goodness or with Sattva guna.

Action that is driven by selfish desires, longing for pleasure, selfishness, enacted with pride and often involves a lot of stress and anxiety is an act of passion and is called Rajasic.

Action that is undertaken because of delusion or ignorance, overlooking consequences and future bondages, without considering loss or injury to others or self, is called Tamasic.

'**Aham**': Clearly, the mix of *Guna* drives one's *Karma* and it also plays a role in determining the suitable pursuits of life. Then what happens when one is asked to perform duties that are not in alignment with one's *Guna*?

'**Brahman**': Yes, *Gunas* are the drivers behind one's desires according to which a person pursues different goals in life. With this learning, you should also realise that **not all duties are equally suited to your current nature**. An ill-suited choice of duty will cause unnecessary strain and resistance[54]. You will realise that it will be extremely difficult for a person with *Tamasic* tendencies to take up the duties of a monk or someone with *Sattvic* qualities to work as a trader who is purely in pursuit of wealth. These are possible scenarios but their work is unlikely to produce the best outcomes as their natural tendencies or qualities are not aligned with their duties. People in such scenarios fail to achieve perfection and remain in stress.

Knowledge of your *Guna* can truly help you understand your personality and outlook. You can use it to align your choice of profession, build a better understanding of your relationship dynamics, better understanding of your behaviour towards your family, friends and colleagues, and even an understanding of your food and lifestyle choices.

'Aham': If I apply the same principles as we discussed in our conversation on *Swadharma* and the pursuits of life then I should try to gravitate towards *Sattvic* qualities and desist *Tamasic* qualities. *Sattvic* qualities will help me stay on the path of *Dharma*. *Rajas* is ok for the pursuit of *Kama* and *Artha* but it will keep me entangled in the desires created by my senses and my ego. *Tamasic* qualities must be restrained and possibly desisted. Is that correct?

---

[54] Remember the importance of Non-Resistance in life as discussed in the chapter on Non-Resistance and Self-Sacrifice.

'Brahman': Yes, you can see that just like we discussed in the case of *Karma Yoga*[55], *Guna* or the *Innate Qualities* are relatable with the pursuits of life. Though, you must also remember that all *Guna* create their own binding effects.

Even *Sattvic* qualities have the tendency to bind you with goodness and spiritual knowledge. That's what *Sattva Guna* stands for. In practical terms, a person with dominant *Sattvic* qualities is likely to be bound by the pursuit of spiritual knowledge and goodness. Binding effects of *Karma* will affect the person as he/she will yearn for creating goodness in the society and attaining further knowledge, even when his/her actions are not driven by desires for personal pleasure and prosperity. This is very similar to what we saw in our discussion on *Karma Yoga*, where acts of *Dharma* are accepted as a great tool for *Nishkama Karma* but they have a tendency to bind oneself to goodness or harmony one creates in the society.

'Aham': Then how do we escape the bondages of *Guna* on the path of *Gyan Yoga*?

'Brahman': We saw that when on the path of *Karma Yoga*, engaging in acts of *Dharma* does not necessarily mean the attainment of *Moksha* or *Liberation* from *Karmic Cycle* and *Suffering*. Similarly, even having pure *Sattvic* qualities won't take you to *Liberation*. At best, it can only help one successfully pursue *Dharma* as a life goal.

---

[55] Discussed in the chapter on "Duty" and "Non-Resistance and Self-Sacrifice".

We discussed that in *Karma yoga*, attainment of *Moksha* is enabled by conscious detachment from all actions including acts of *Dharma* and goodness created by them. That kind of complete detachment and self-abnegation helps attain *Moksha* on the path of *Karma Yoga*. On the path of self-knowledge or *Gyan Yoga*, the final frontier of attaining *Moksha* is achieved when you are clearly able to comprehend that your *Guna* is driving all your actions, and you have the realisation that your *Guna* is separate from your 'true' self. This is the state when you have transcended all *Guna* and can see yourself as separate from your *Guna*.

प्रकृतेः क्रियमाणानि गुणैः कर्माणि सर्वशः |
अहङ्कारविमूढात्मा कर्ताहमिति मन्यते ||

Bhagavad Gita chapter 3 verse 27

All activities are carried out by the three Guna (natural qualities or tendencies) of material nature. But in ignorance, the soul, deluded by false identification with the body, thinks itself to be the doer.

'**Aham**': You are saying that when true knowledge is attained and one realises the 'true' self, then there is no association with one's basic nature? My likes and dislikes are not mine? Who am I then?

'**Brahman**': When you can see your 'self' separate from your *Guna*, you have the realisation of your 'true' self.

You have seen how *Avidya* and *Guna* keep you engaged in the binding effects of *Karma* and trapped in *Māyā*. You are now also aware of the knowledge or realisation that is missing. Let's now look deeper into the path of *Gyan Yoga* so that you understand how to pursue that 'knowledge' or that 'realisation'.

Chapter 12 - True Self: Brahman

'Aham': I am still not convinced with what you said at the end of our last conversation about self-realisation and *Guna*. *Guna* being our basic innate qualities, how can one transcend these or detach from one's *Guna*? Can it really happen? If yes, then how? What triggers it?

'Brahman': Ok let me explain to you how to pursue the path of *Gyan Yoga* which will help answer your queries.

Earlier, we discussed *Karma Yoga* as a way to *Moksha,* navigating through life while performing one's *Personal Duties*. We also discussed *Bhakti Yoga* as the path to *Moksha,* suited for those who tread the path of devotion and worship. *Gyan Yoga*, on the other hand, is a path of contemplation, analysis and self-inquiry. The journey on the path of *Gyan Yoga* is the one of self-realisation.

As I warned earlier, this path of self-realisation is likely to take you to unfamiliar territories. It involves a lot of thinking, contemplation and analysis of things in life that you have always taken for granted. This is about asking some truly profound questions about your own being. Just like the other two yoga - *Karma* and *Bhakti, Gyan Yoga* is all about practice. It's not about taking my words as gospel. No teaching or words of wisdom can substitute your own realisation. With that in mind, let me take you to the point up to which words can serve. Beyond that, it will be your own journey of self-inquiry.

वस्तुस्वरूपं स्फुटबोधचक्षुषा
स्वेनैव वेद्यं न तु पण्डितेन ।
चन्द्रस्वरूपं निजचक्षुषैव
ज्ञातव्यमन्यैरवगम्यते किम् ॥

Vivekachudamani - Verse 54

The true nature of Reality is to be known by first-hand personal experience through the eye of clear understanding, and not through the report of learned men. The beauty of the moon is enjoyed through one's own eyes. Can one appreciate it through someone else's description?

Many different ways have been suggested to undertake the process of self-inquiry so that you can see your 'true' self. When I had asked you earlier to identify yourself, you chose many different identities that you associate with. Mostly you identified with your body, mind, thoughts, personality, and possessions.

Think about your body - say, your limbs, what happens if you surgically replace a limb? You will still identify with yourself. You will know who has lost a limb. Isn't it? What if your kidney or heart is transplanted? You will still know who you are.

Your possessions can keep changing over time, but there is something in you that stays all along irrespective of what you possess. That one is aware of what you possess and what you don't. Thus, possessions can't be fundamental to your existence.

Your thoughts and personality also change over time. Who is the witness to that change? What is it that remains as a witness while your thoughts and personality undergo various changes?

You may feel that it's your mind that controls everything else - body, thoughts and feelings. Well, have you ever tried to sit in silence observing your mind? Have you been able to see your mind wandering from one thought to another, from one analysis to another? What is it that observes the wandering mind?

The one thing that is common amongst all the above cases is that there is something in you because of which you are aware or conscious of those other claimed identities. That awareness or consciousness lies deep inside you and holds all your claimed identities. Do you remember our conversation on identity when I said I am interested in knowing your deepest self, the canvas on which you paint the identities associated with your body, mind, thoughts, personality and possessions[56]? This is what we are getting down to.

'Aham': I can make some sense of it. Clearly, you are after the most fundamental aspect of my being. However, I don't think I completely understand the concept of consciousness. Are you saying that I am nothing else but awareness or consciousness? Also,

---

[56] This topic was   discussed in the chapter on *Maya* and *Avidya*.

why not associate with the identities that I have claimed? What's the harm in associating with my body, my mind, my thoughts, my religion, my language, my country, my beliefs, and so on?

'Brahman': We have already discussed the ill-effects of identifying with your body, mind, thoughts and so on when we talked about *Avidya*. Identifying with such finite, perishable and destructible entities immediately makes you a selfish person who wants to preserve and protect what one identifies with. They create all sorts of attachments that eventually bring *Suffering* and *Misery* in your life. This is the direct and most visible impact of *Avidya* that you can see in your life as you associate with or feel attached to those claimed identities.

न प्रमादादनर्थोऽन्यो ज्ञानिनः स्वस्वरूपतः ।
ततो मोहस्ततोऽहंधीस्ततो बन्धस्ततो व्यथा ॥

Vivekachudamani - Verse 322

For the wise, there is no greater danger than ignorance of one's own real nature. From this comes delusion; from delusion comes egoism; from egoism comes bondage/attachments; and from bondage comes misery.

Now that you can see how *Avidya* or ignorance about 'self' manifests in your life and directly leads you to *Suffering* and *Misery*, let's look at ways of removing this ignorance. Ignorance is always removed by knowledge and in this case, it is - self-knowledge.

This is an attempt to know and realise your 'true' self.

'Aham': Please guide me through discovering my 'true' self on the path of *Gyan Yoga*.

'Brahman': Sure. Carrying on how we analysed your various claimed identities, let's have another go at it but this time with a bit more structured approach to uncovering the 'true' you!

In this process, we will look at how you experience yourself and the world. All your experiences will have two things in common - an experiencer and an experienced, in other words - a seer and a seen. The ultimate experiencer or the seer or the observer is what we are interested in. Focus on the subject - who is it that is experiencing or observing?
And of course, the other part would be the one that is seen or observed or experienced. This is the object of the experience – think, what is it that is being experienced or observed?

Distinguish between the 'observer' and the 'observed', the 'seer' and the 'seen', the 'experiencer' and the 'experienced' and keep the focus on the subject i.e. the observer or the seer or the experiencer. We will employ a process called *Neti Neti* - Not this, Not this, or a negation strategy to negate everything that you are not. In the end, you should be left with something that you are. Through this experiment, let's try to establish the nature of your 'true' self who is the ultimate experiencer or the observer or the witness. You don't need to believe any doctrine or dogma. Just keep faith in your own experiences. We will take an outside-in approach or go from the outside world to somewhere within you - just like we peel the layers of an onion, and hopefully find your 'true' self somewhere in this journey.

Let's start with the world, anything in the entire universe other than your body and mind. The distant stars, the sky, the trees, the river, the buildings, the furniture and so on. You can observe them, experience them. You are the experiencer; they are the experienced. You are the observer; they are the observed. The outside world is not you. Who is experiencing it? Who is observing?

You experience that outside world with your body and sense organs - you can touch them, see them, smell and feel them. So is it your body who is the experiencer or the observer?

Now let's look at your gross body - your hands, your legs, your face, etc. You can again see them, touch them, feel them, use them! You can experience and interact with your own body. Of course, your sense-organs and mind can help you observe and perceive your gross body. That means you are not your gross body as it is experienced and observed by you.

So are you your sense-organs - eyes, ears, nose, tongue and skin? Well, you are always aware of these organs. These simply sense the outside world for you. They are not you. They are rather serving you and you can observe them doing their job for you.

Then let's go a step deeper, maybe it's the subtle internal organs that are the true experiencers of everything else. Well, even that is not the case. You can sense your internal organs as well. Your heart beats quite distinctly. Many other organs such as liver, stomach, kidney, and others have their own way of making themselves known to you, especially when something goes wrong! So once again, you can observe, sense, feel the organs within you. They are the 'known' and you are the 'knower'. They are the 'observed' and you are the 'observer'.

Then you can say that it's the mind that processes all sensations. Also, it is the mind where all the thoughts arise, where all the analysis is done and where memories are created. But we have already discussed how you can be aware of your thoughts, feelings, and analysis. With little discrimination, you would be able to witness all the thoughts and emotions in your own mind, thereby becoming a witness to your mind itself. You can observe the thoughts and analysis going on in your mind. There is still an experiencer or observer or witness within you that is separate from the thoughts, analysis, feelings and memories of your mind. So mind and its products are the 'known' and you are the 'knower'. There is an awareness that enables you to experience all that goes on in your mind.

Then what about the blank mind? Mind that is thoughtless. You are always in one of the three states - the waking state, the dreaming sleep and the dreamless sleep. Waking state is when you are actively experiencing the world through your body and mind. You are aware or conscious of that state. In the dreaming state of sleep, you are not actively using your body but your mind is actively creating dreams. You are still aware of what your mind is doing. The consciousness persists. But what happens when you are in dreamless sleep, which is known as deep sleep when the activities of the mind shut down as well? There is nothing to experience but your consciousness is still there that eventually makes you aware of that nothingness.

यो विजानाति सकलं जाग्रत्स्वप्नसुषुप्तिषु ।
बुद्धितद्वृत्तिसद्भावमभावमहमित्ययम् ॥

Vivekachudamani - Verse 126

That which knows everything that happens in the waking, dream, and deep-sleep states. That which is aware of the presence or absence of the mind and its functions. That which is the essence behind the ego. That is —This—the Self.

This is all boiling down to the fact that it's the consciousness or awareness that experiences everything else - from the outside world to your body to your mind, feelings, intellect, thoughts and even the absence of thoughts is witnessed through awareness.

Can you go any deeper than that? Is there anything with which you can witness the awareness itself?

'Aham': I am not sure. Perhaps not.

'Brahman': Is there anything that you can experience or witness that is not in your awareness or consciousness?

'Aham': No, it can't be. If something is not in my awareness then how can it be known to me or be experienced by me?

'Brahman': True. This is a purely empirical experiment that we have done together. Verified through your own experiences. I hope you can see that at the very depth of your own self what lies is pure consciousness or awareness, and everything else is an object in your awareness. It's this consciousness that helps you experience all that there is.

With the process of *Neti Neti* - Not this, Not this, or a negation strategy we have actively negated everything that you are not. In the end, you can see that all you are left with is consciousness or awareness.

'Aham': Yes, I understand that but does that mean my true self is pure consciousness? Is that what I am? What's the role of the life within me then? Maybe that life force within me is my 'true' self. Consciousness depends on life. Isn't it?

'Brahman': We have started to talk about life and death now. You may say that if life is not there then there is no question of consciousness or awareness. So consciousness is dependent upon life. There can be a few counter-arguments to this. A logical challenge would be that in your experience or anybody's experience, there is never a moment when there is no consciousness. There could be moments when there are no bodily or worldly experiences in your consciousness, for example in deep sleep, but it doesn't prove the absence of consciousness. However, is this the same in the case of death? Unfortunately, it isn't easy to check for consciousness post-death! However, as medical science has progressed, many cases of conscious experiences have been shared by people who came out of a coma or even from death post-resuscitation. These were patients who have shared very lucid and vivid memories of times just after death.

'Aham': I am aware of such studies that have been done. A widely reported study by Dr Sam Parnia was published in 2014 called AWARE — the awareness during resuscitation trial, the world's largest study of what happens to the human mind and consciousness just after death.

'Brahman': There you go. You have evidence of consciousness, but you have no evidence of a point in time when it wasn't there or a point when it won't be there in future. This is what all your experience and even science can tell you today.

However, the ultimate proof would come to you when you have realised it yourself. Then there would be no doubts remaining.

'Aham': Perhaps you are right. We are talking about something which definitely exists today but there is no evidence of its birth and its death. I can try to argue that consciousness is born with the body and it dies with the body, but I would not be able to furnish any evidence to support it. All that can be said is that it exists, it has existed and it will exist.

It still feels strange as I have never conceived my 'self' as consciousness. Why do we normally see ourselves so differently then, in terms of our body, mind, thoughts, possessions, attachments, and so on?

Why do we have this ignorance, to begin with? And then, what happens when we start to identify with consciousness?

'Brahman': *Avidya* or ignorance about self always exists and so does *Māyā*, as we had discussed earlier. You can't attribute a beginning to ignorance. When you are ignorant of something, there is no fixed beginning of that ignorance. It's always there. You can test it for anything you are ignorant of. Say, the laws of quantum mechanics. If you are ignorant of them then that's how it has always been. Yes, ignorance can be removed so it can have a definite end and ignorance is removed by knowledge. In this case, *Avidya* or ignorance about self is removed by the knowledge of 'true' self.

We have discussed a few times how under the influence of *Avidya* you identify with your ego-self, which in turn has the tendency to create attachments with the help of your senses and ego-driven mind. When there is no ego-self there is no question of attachments. With no attachments, consciousness shines clear.

Let me briefly explain to you what I mean by that. Your mind and your senses are great instruments to perceive this world. This applies to every bit in this world - ideas, thoughts, objects, beings, relationships, everything. The issue is that your perceptions are coloured by your attachments. Say, if you like being in the wild, a chance to walk through a national park could look really appealing to you but it may not be perceived in the same way by another person who has a different taste in life. So the situation is exactly the same but two people will perceive them very differently based on their own likes and dislikes and attachments. The same phenomenon occurs in every situation and everything that you face in life. You never perceive or experience things as they are but you only do so through your attachments. Whatever you are seeing, perceiving, judging, experiencing is being influenced by your attachments. This is why it's said that you don't see the true reality and you allow *Māyā* to exist.

On the contrary, when you identify with consciousness, the ignorance of ego-self doesn't exist anymore. Remember consciousness is pure awareness without any prejudices or likes and dislikes. Its only function is to be aware or conscious of any and all experiences without giving them any particular colour or flavour. As ego-self disappears and so do the attachments, you begin to see things and situations purely as they are. You begin to see the true reality.

This is what begins to happen when you identify with consciousness rather than your ego-self.

'Aham': I can see how this path of self-realisation and identifying with consciousness rather than the ego-self leads to non-attachment and that helps to see the world in its truest sense. I am also able to relate it to our discussion on *Karma Yoga*, as the path of *Swadharma* and *Non-Resistance* becomes clearer as my attachments drop through self-realisation.

'Brahman': Yes, you are thinking in the right direction but let me warn you that to get rid of *Avidya* there is a big obstacle that you need to overcome. Just the knowledge of your 'true' self is not enough. **This knowledge has to be 'realized' or 'experienced'.** You would have heard a story of an elephant who was tied with a brittle chain all its life and even as an adult it never broke the chain. The elephant saw the chain every day, felt it, played with it, but never broke it. Just the knowledge of the brittle chain is never enough. Even your own power has to be realised. The same effects are also seen in sports psychology and a great deal of time and effort is put in by players to realise one's potential. It's the same principle that applies to realising your 'true' self as well. This knowledge of 'true' self is the first step but ultimately it has to be realised.

अज्ञानयोगात्परमात्मनस्तव
ह्यनात्मबन्धस्तत एव संसृतिः ।
तयोर्विवेकोदितबोधवन्हिः
अज्ञानकार्यं प्रदहेत्समूलम् ॥

Vivekachudamani, verse 47

You are indeed the supreme Self but due to your association with ignorance you find yourself under the bondage of the non-self, which is the sole cause of the cycle of births and deaths. All the effects of ignorance, root and branch, are burnt down by the fire of knowledge (when gained from own experience), which arises from discrimination between these two—the Self and the non-Self.

'**Aham**': Well, I can understand that realisation is still a conscious step that one needs to take. Though, please tell me more about the nature of 'true' self - the nature of my consciousness.

'**Brahman**': Look, you have committed the most

critical mistake already. **Remember that it's not 'your' consciousness, you 'are' consciousness**. This is what happens when you still associate with your mind and try to look at consciousness through your mind. You will be able to differentiate between the two when you have realised the 'true' nature of self. Without self-realisation, all that I say will only remain a theoretical concept for you, like a gospel.

Treat this knowledge as a pointer that directionally shows you what your 'true' self is, but then don't focus on this knowledge, focus on self-realisation. Once you have realised your 'true' self, you will not need this pointer (or knowledge) any more.

Let me explain this with an example. Do you remember when you were learning to ride a bicycle for the first time? It's the same concept. I can give you endless lectures on how to ride a bicycle and how to coordinate your body and mind to maintain balance while riding. However, you can't ride a bicycle successfully just with that knowledge. Or no knowledge can help you experience the joy of riding a bicycle. Riding has to be your own experience. Very importantly, once you ride the bicycle successfully, you will not need any theory or lectures whatsoever on how to coordinate your body and mind to balance the bicycle. It's just known to you. In the same way, once you have realised your 'true' self you will not need any of this knowledge any more.

Suppose a thorn has pierced a man's foot. He picks another thorn to pull out the first one. After extracting the first thorn with the help of the second, he throws

120

both away. One should use the thorn of knowledge to pull out the thorn of ignorance. Then both the thorns should be thrown away.

- Teachings of Ramkrishna Paramhansa

'Aham': I understand that but please share with me the knowledge so that I can use it as a guide or a pointer, as you say, in my own pursuit of self-realisation.

'Brahman': Ok let me end this by briefly describing to you the nature of consciousness.

- Consciousness is pure existence, pure awareness.

- Consciousness is all-pervading. Everything - matter, life, energy, in the universe is part of consciousness. It pervades everything that "exists".

- Consciousness is without beginning and has no end either. It is neither born nor dies. It is eternal.

- Consciousness is infinite or non-ending and non-dual.

- You are pure consciousness and pure consciousness is *Brahman*.

तस्य हेतुरविद्या,
तदभावात्संयोगाभावो हानं तद् दृशेः कैवल्यम् ।
Yoga Sutra (Sadhana Pada), 2:24-25

After the dissolution of avidya (ignorance), comes removal of communion with the material world. This is the path to Kaivalyam (Moksha).

This is self-realisation, realisation that you are pure consciousness, realisation that you are *Brahman*. This self-realisation removes *Avidya* and leads to *Moksha* on the path of *Gyan Yoga*.

The Four Maha-Vakyas - "The Great Sayings" of the Upanishad

Prajnanam Brahma – Brahman is consciousness.
(Aitareya Upanishad 3.3 of the Rig Veda)

Aham Brahmasmi – I am Brahman.
(Mandukya Upanishad 1.2 of the Atharva Veda)

Tat Tvam Asi – Thou art that.
(Chandogya Upanishad 6.8.7 of the Sama Veda)

Ayam Atma Brahma – Atman (true 'self') is Brahman.
(Brihadaranyaka Upanishad 1.4.10 of the Yajur Veda)

Glossary

Advaita Vedanta - (/əd.'vaɪ.tə vɛd'antə/ Sanskrit: अद्वैत वेदान्त) is a sub-school within the ancient orthodox school of Vedanta. It reflects ideas that emerged from the philosophies contained in the Upanishads, the Brahma Sutras and the Bhagavad Gita. The Advaita school believes that *Brahman* is the one and only reality and everything else including individual beings are reflection of projection of *Brahman*.

Adharma - not in alignment or not in conformity with *Dharma*.

Aham or *Ahamkara* - (Sanskrit: अहंकार) ego-self or the identification and attachment with one's ego.

Apara Bhakti - a lower form of *Bhakti* where the devotee worships one or more *Personal God(s)* to fulfil one's desires or out of fear.

Ājīvika - is one of the *Nāstika* schools of Indian philosophy, purportedly founded in the 5th century BC by Makkhali Gosala.

Astika – ancient philosophies that originated from the Indian sub-continent that were based on the Veda.

Avidya - ignorance of true-self. Refer chapter 10 Maya and Avidya.

Bhakta - follower of *Bhakti Yoga*.

Bhakti - love and devotion.

Bhakti Yoga - path of attainment of *Moksha* through love and devotion. Refer chapter 9 - Path of Love.

Brahman - the ultimate or absolute reality. Also, referred to as Supreme Consciousness, Supreme God. Refer chapter 12 – True Self: Brahman.

Cārvāka - (Sanskrit: चार्वाक), also known as Lokāyata, is an ancient school of Indian materialism and is considered part of the Nastika group of philosophies.

Dharma - (/'dɑːrmə/; Sanskrit: धर्म) is derived from the root dhṛ, which means to hold, maintain or keep. *Dharma* relates to the law or order that keeps the world or the universe functioning in peace and harmony.

Dharmic - aligned or in conformity with *Dharma*.

Gyan Yoga - also written as *Jñāna Yoga*, is the path to attainment of *Moksha* through self-knowledge or self-realisation.

Guna - refer Chapter 11 - *Guna (Innate Qualities)*

Guru – teacher/guide.

Ignorance - see *Avidya*.

Innate Qualities - see *Guna*.

Ishta Devta - The word Ishta is derived from the root

Ish, to desire, choose. Ishta Devta is a god of one's own choosing that's why it's also called Personal God. In Hinduism, many forms of Gods have been referenced that are often called deities, celestial gods, etc. and each of them typically represent certain values, personality and power. This helps devotees to initially engage with and focus on a form of God which naturally aligns with their thoughts and desires. For example, Goddess Laxmi is often worshipped by those who desire wealth and prosperity. Refer chapter 9 – Path of Love.

Jñāna Yoga - see *Gyan Yoga*.

Kāma - (Sanskrit: काम) means desire, wish or longing. It's one of the four acceptable pursuits of human life (Puruṣārtha) as long as it is not pursued at the expense of the other three. In general, it relates to all kinds of desires, passion or longing for pleasure of the senses, the aesthetic pleasures of life, affection, love, sexual, sensual and erotic pleasures, and so on.

Karma - (/ˈkɑːrmə/; Sanskrit: कर्म) means action, work or deed. *Karma* includes three types of actions - kāyik (performed with the body or limbs), vāchik (performed by speaking), and mānasik (performed by the mind - thoughts, analysis, feelings).

Karma-Phal - Returns/Rewards of *Karma*. For example, say, you are shooting at a target to win a prize. Here, shooting is the action or *Karma*, hitting the bull's eye is the result or effect of the action and getting the prize money is the Return/Reward of the action i.e. *Karma-Phal.*

Karma Yoga - path of attainment of *Moksha* by carrying out one's *Personal Duties* or *Swadharma*.

Karma Yogi - one who treads the path of *Karma Yoga*.

Karmic Cycle — attachments create desires and desires create motives or intentions that subsequently drive one's *Karma*. Every act undertaken to fulfil a desire creates a binding effect that further reinforces the original desire (or attachment) and then influences future actions as well. This self-reinforcing cycle is called *Karmic Cycle*. Acting with detachment while following *Swadharma* helps to break the *Karmic cycle*.

Kaurava - the 100 sons of the King of Hastinapur, Dhritarashtra, and his wife Gandhari who fought the battle of *Kurukshetra* in the epic, Mahabharata, against their cousins *Pandava*.

Kurukshetra - is the place where the final war described in the Hindu epic poem *Mahābhārata* was fought. The conflict arose from a dynastic succession struggle between two groups of cousins, the *Kaurava* and the *Pandava*.

Law of Karma - The *Law of Karma*, also known as the law of causation, is a universal law which simply means every action will have a commensurate effect. Refer to chapter 5 on the *Law of Karma*.

Liberation - see *Moksha*.

Mahābhārata - literally means "Great Epic of the Bharata Dynasty". It is one of the two Sanskrit epic poems of ancient India (the other being the Ramayana). The Mahābhārata is an epic that narrates the struggle between two groups of cousins - the Kaurava and the Pāṇḍava princes. It's marked by the famous battle of Kurukshetra and the revered Bhagavad Gita.

Māyā - explained in the chapter on *Māyā* and *Avidya*.

Moksha - (/ˈmoʊkʃə/; Sanskrit: मोक्ष) is the ultimate pursuit of human life leading to liberation from all attachments and the binding effects of *Karma*. It's a state of eternal calm and bliss.

Nāstika - Ancient philosophies that originated from the Indian sub-continent that were not based on the *Veda*.

Natural Tendencies - see Guna.

Neti Neti - Not this, Not this. Refer chapter 12 - True Self: Brahman

Nishkāma Karma - *Karma* that is not driven by selfish desires.

Non-Resistance - refer chapter 8 - Non-Resistance and Self-Sacrifice.

Pandava - the five powerful and skilled sons of Pandu and his two wives Kunti and Madri. The *Pandavas* - Yudhistira, Bhima, Arjuna, Nakula, and Sahadeva - fought the war of *Kurukshetra* against their cousins, the *Kauravas*.

Para Bhakti - highest form of *Bhakti* when a *Bhakta* feels a sense of oneness with *Brahman*.

Personal God - see *Ishta Devta*.

Personal Duties – see *Swadharma*.

Puruṣārtha - acceptable pursuits of human life.

Rajas - refer chapter 11 - *Guna* (*Innate Qualities*).

Sattva - refer chapter 11 - *Guna* (*Innate Qualities*).

Sanatana Dharma - eternal way of life. Refer chapter 1 – Introduction.

Sindhu - river Indus.

Suffering and Misery - refer chapter 2 – Attachments and Desires.

Swadharma - one's own *Dharma* or one's own set of duties. Refer chapter 7 – Duty.

Tamas - refer chapter 11 - *Guna* (*Innate Qualities*).

Upanishad - (/uːˈpɑːnɪ ʃɑːd/; Sanskrit: उपनिषद्) are part of *Veda* and relate to the ideas and teachings of meditation, philosophy, and spiritual knowledge.

Vedanta - (/vɪˈdɑːntə/; Sanskrit: वेदान्त) is one of the six (*āstika*) schools of Hindu philosophy. Literally meaning "end of the Vedas", it reflects the philosophies contained in the Upanishads.

Veda - (Sanskrit: वेद, literal translation - "knowledge") are a large body of religious texts written in vedic Sanskrit in ancient India. There are four Veda: the Rigveda, the Yajurveda, the Samaveda and the Atharvaveda. Each Veda has been subclassified into four major parts – the Samhitas (mantras, hymns and benedictions), the Aranyakas (text on philosophy behind rituals and sacrifices), the Brahmanas (commentaries on the performance of rituals, and sacrifices), and the Upanishads (discussions on meditation, philosophy and spiritual knowledge).

Yoga - (/ˈjoʊɡə/; Sanskrit: योग) means union. Note that it may bear different meanings depending upon the context. Yoga is one of the six *Āstika* schools of Hindu philosophical traditions. It also means 'path' when used in conjunction with, say, *Karma*, *Bhakti*, etc. to denote different paths to *Moksha*.

Printed in Great Britain
by Amazon